Editorial project:
© 2025 **booq** publishing, S.L.
c/ Domènech, 7-9, 2º 1ª
08012 Barcelona, Spain
T: +34 93 268 80 88
www.booqpublishing.com

ISBN: 978-8499-36-586-2 [EN]
ISBN: 978-8499-36-582-4 [ES]

Editorial coordinator:
Claudia Martínez Alonso

Layout:
Cristina Simó Perales

Translation:
© **booq** publishing, S.L.

Printing in China

Until the late nineteenth century, Scandinavian Architecture was based on vernacular wooden, stone, and brick structures constructed by those without formal architectural training. Although unheralded, they offered practical solutions to problems specific to the north, including maximizing natural light and heat during the dark, cold winter days.
Nordic Architecture is nowadays functional, attractive in a minimalist way, and in balance with nature. At the same time, architects play a role in the emergence of the region's social welfare model, which requires quality in housing and public buildings. With more than 400 illustrations and floor plans, this book provides a visual introduction of the most relevant architects in the region, showing how Scandinavian architects use their own resources and traditions to generate ideas that currently influence other international firms.

Bis ins späte neunzehnte Jahrhundert stützte sich die skandinavische Architektur auf Holz-, Stein- und Ziegelbauten, die im Volksmund von Menschen ohne formale Architekturausbildung errichtet wurden. Obwohl sie nicht angekündigt waren, boten sie praktische Lösungen für spezifische Probleme des Nordens, einschließlich der Maximierung von natürlichem Licht und Wärme während der dunklen, kalten Wintertage. Die nordische Architektur ist heute funktional, auf minimalistische Weise attraktiv und im Gleichgewicht mit der Natur. Gleichzeitig spielen Architekten eine Rolle bei der Entstehung des sozialen Wohlfahrtsmodells der Region, das Qualität im Wohnungsbau und bei öffentlichen Gebäuden erfordert.
Mit mehr als 400 Abbildungen und Grundrissen bietet dieses Buch eine visuelle Einführung in die wichtigsten Architekten der Region und zeigt, wie skandinavische Architekten ihre eigenen Ressourcen und Traditionen nutzen, um Ideen zu entwickeln, die derzeit andere internationale Firmen beeinflussen.

Jusqu'à la fin du XIXe siècle, l'architecture scandinave était basée sur des structures vernaculaires en bois, en pierre et en brique construites par des personnes sans formation architecturale formelle. Bien qu'elles n'aient pas été annoncées, elles offraient des solutions pratiques aux problèmes spécifiques au Nord, notamment l'optimisation de la lumière et de la chaleur naturelles pendant les jours sombres et froids de l'hiver.
L'architecture nordique est aujourd'hui fonctionnelle, attrayante de manière minimaliste et en équilibre avec la nature. En même temps, les architectes jouent un rôle dans l'émergence du modèle de bien-être social de la région, qui exige la qualité des logements et des bâtiments publics. Avec plus de 400 illustrations et plans, ce livre fournit une introduction visuelle des architectes les plus importants de la région, montrant comment les architectes scandinaves utilisent leurs propres ressources et traditions pour générer des idées qui influencent actuellement d'autres cabinets internationaux.

Hasta finales del siglo XIX, la arquitectura escandinava se basaba en estructuras vernáculas de madera, piedra y ladrillo construidas por personas sin formación arquitectónica formal. Aunque no se anunciaban, ofrecían soluciones prácticas a los problemas específicos del norte, incluyendo la maximización de la luz natural y el calor durante los oscuros y fríos días de invierno.
La arquitectura nórdica es hoy en día funcional, atractiva de forma minimalista y en equilibrio con la naturaleza. Al mismo tiempo, los arquitectos desempeñan un papel en el surgimiento del modelo de bienestar social de la región, que exige calidad en la vivienda y en los edificios públicos. Con más de 400 ilustraciones y planos, este libro ofrece una introducción visual de los arquitectos más relevantes de la región, mostrando cómo los arquitectos escandinavos utilizan sus propios recursos y tradiciones para generar ideas que actualmente influyen en otras firmas internacionales.

CABIN RISØR

CABIN RISØR

Risør, Norway
Photos: © Jan Roger Bodin, Margaret M. de Lange

The summer cabin is located on a small island close to Risør on the south-eastern coast of Norway. An old cottage was sited at the island´s mid-point. The client asked for a new cabin as replacement for the old one. The new cabin is placed in the same mid-point with an outdoor atrium as a nave for all activities. All rooms are directly connected to the atrium. The building wraps around the atrium thus giving shelter for outdoor meals and calm activities. The rooms have selected views to the surrounding sea, fjord and close nature with smooth cliffs and pinetrees. The living rooms and kitchen also meet the cliffs outside on a lower level that opens towards the sea in northwest, evening sun and sunset. A colonnade along the front has specially designed moveable screens that protects the indoor spaces from the hot evening sun and gives a semi-transparent play of light and shadow to the rooms.

Die Sommerhütte befindet sich auf einer kleinen Insel in der Nähe von Risør an der südöstlichen Küste Norwegens. Eine alte Konstruktion stand zuvor in der Mitte der Insel. Der Kunde wünschte eine neue Hütte als Ersatz für das Original. Die neue Hütte wurde an derselben Stelle errichtet, mit einem zentralen Außenatrium, an das alle Räume angeschlossen sind. Die Konstruktion umschließt das Atrium und bietet Schutz für Mahlzeiten im Freien und ruhige Aktivitäten. Die Räume bieten ausgewählte Ausblicke auf das umliegende Meer, den Fjord und die nahe Natur mit sanften Klippen und Kiefern. Das Wohnzimmer und die Küche öffnen sich auf einer niedrigeren Ebene zu den Außenklippen hin und sind nach Nordwesten ausgerichtet, sodass die Abendsonne und der Sonnenuntergang sichtbar werden. Eine Kolonnade entlang der Hauptfassade ist mit speziell entworfenen beweglichen Paneelen ausgestattet, die die Innenräume vor der intensiven Abendsonne schützen und ein halbtransparentes Spiel aus Licht und Schatten in den Räumen erzeugen.

La cabane d'été est située sur une petite île près de Risør, sur la côte sud-est de la Norvège. Une ancienne construction se trouvait au centre de l'île. Le client a demandé une nouvelle cabane pour remplacer l'originale. La nouvelle construction est implantée au même endroit, avec un atrium extérieur comme axe central auquel toutes les pièces sont reliées. La structure entoure l'atrium, offrant un abri pour les repas en plein air et les activités calmes. Les pièces bénéficient de vues choisies sur la mer environnante, le fjord et la nature environnante, avec de douces falaises et des pins. Le salon et la cuisine s'ouvrent sur les falaises extérieures à un niveau inférieur, orienté au nord-ouest, permettant l'entrée du soleil de l'après-midi et offrant une vue sur le coucher du soleil. Une colonnade le long de la façade principale est dotée de panneaux mobiles spécialement conçus pour protéger les espaces intérieurs du soleil intense du soir, créant un jeu semi-transparent de lumière et d'ombre dans les pièces.

La cabaña de verano está ubicada en una pequeña isla cerca de Risør, en la costa sureste de Noruega. Una antigua construcción estaba situada en el punto medio de la isla. El cliente solicitó una nueva para reemplazar la original. La nueva cabaña se ubica en el mismo punto medio, con un atrio exterior como eje central al que se conectan todas las habitaciones. La construcción envuelve el atrio, proporcionando resguardo para comidas al aire libre y actividades tranquilas. Las habitaciones cuentan con vistas seleccionadas al mar circundante, al fiordo y a la naturaleza cercana, con suaves acantilados y pinos. La sala de estar y la cocina se abren a los acantilados exteriores en un nivel inferior, orientado al noroeste, permitiendo la entrada del sol de la tarde y la vista del atardecer. Una columnata a lo largo de la fachada principal cuenta con paneles móviles diseñados especialmente para proteger los espacios interiores del intenso sol vespertino, creando un juego semitransparente de luz y sombra en las habitaciones.

ARK-TELLUS

Reinterpreting local traditions, a summer retreat was created where architecture and landscape blend seamlessly around a sanctuary with a central atrium.

VILLA ROSANES

VILLA ROSANES

Nøtterøy, Norway
Photos: © Jan Roger Bodin, Espen Grønli

The villa is a complete remodelling of a residence from the 1920s. It was originally a Jugend-style villa, but has since been refurbished several times. With larger construction-parts damaged, a major reconstruction was required. The client asked for reconstruction which would relate to the environment consisting of classic villas, but with a contemporary interpretation. The new design preserves the main structure and retains the place on site with it´s characteristic volume and profile. The entrance, ground plan and interior has been relocated and the upper attic removed, so that the first floor has got spacious rooms underneath the pitched roof. The whole exterior of the building is clad in cedarwood and given precise detailing. Important achievements of the design has been to open up and strengthen the contact between outside and inside spaces, and provide a good flow between the different living rooms.

Die Villa ist eine umfassende Renovierung eines Wohnhauses aus den 1920er Jahren. Ursprünglich war es eine Jugendstil-Villa, die jedoch im Laufe der Jahre mehrfach umgebaut wurde. Aufgrund struktureller Schäden war eine umfangreiche Rekonstruktion erforderlich. Der Kunde wünschte eine Renovierung, die sich in das klassische Villen-Umfeld einfügt, jedoch mit einer zeitgenössischen Interpretation. Das neue Design bewahrt die Hauptstruktur und die ursprüngliche Lage des Gebäudes, respektiert dessen Volumen und charakteristisches Profil. Der Eingang, die Raumaufteilung und das Innere wurden neu organisiert, und das obere Dachgeschoss wurde entfernt, um im ersten Stock großzügige Räume unter dem Giebeldach zu ermöglichen. Die gesamte Außenverkleidung besteht aus Zedernholz und weist präzise Details auf. Ein zentrales Ziel des Entwurfs war es, die Verbindung zwischen Innen- und Außenräumen zu öffnen und zu stärken, um einen guten Fluss zwischen den verschiedenen Wohnbereichen zu schaffen.

La villa est une rénovation complète d'une résidence des années 1920. À l'origine, il s'agissait d'une villa de style Jugend, mais elle a été rénovée à plusieurs reprises. Avec certaines parties structurelles endommagées, une reconstruction majeure a été nécessaire. Le client souhaitait une rénovation en accord avec l'environnement des villas classiques, mais avec une interprétation contemporaine. Le nouveau design conserve la structure principale et maintient son emplacement d'origine, respectant son volume et son profil caractéristique. L'entrée, la disposition des pièces et l'intérieur ont été repensés, et les combles supérieurs ont été supprimés, permettant au premier étage d'avoir de grandes pièces sous le toit à deux pans. L'ensemble de la façade extérieure est revêtu de bois de cèdre et comporte des détails précis. Un objectif clé du projet a été d'ouvrir et de renforcer le lien entre les espaces intérieurs et extérieurs, offrant une fluidité entre les différentes zones de vie.

La villa es una remodelación completa de una residencia de la década de 1920. Originalmente era una villa de estilo Jugend, pero ha sido renovada en varias ocasiones. Con partes estructurales dañadas, se requirió una reconstrucción importante. El cliente pidió una reforma que mantuviera relación con el entorno de villas clásicas, pero con una interpretación contemporánea. El nuevo diseño conserva la estructura principal y mantiene su ubicación original, respetando su volumen y perfil característico. La entrada, la distribución en planta y el interior han sido reubicados, y la buhardilla superior eliminada, permitiendo que la primera planta cuente con habitaciones amplias bajo el techo a dos aguas. Todo el exterior del edificio está revestido en madera de cedro y cuenta con detalles precisos. Un objetivo clave del diseño ha sido abrir y fortalecer el vínculo entre los espacios interiores y exteriores, proporcionando un buen flujo entre las diferentes áreas de estar.

ARK-TELLUS

FAMILY HOUSE EKELUNDEN

FAMILY HOUSE EKELUNDEN

Tjøme, Norway
Photos: © Jan Roger Bodin, Espen Grønli

The house is situated in the characteristic landscape of Tjøme, an island by the Oslofjord. The small existing farmhouse dates from 1870 and is well preserved. The client asked for an extension twice the size of the original 50 square metre house. The client and the architects found a common passion for nature and landscaping. The site is located in a lush broad-leaved forest with characteristic smooth cliffs which raise from the forest floor like the back of a whale breaking the waves. The architects recognised the challenge of new expressions meeting the vernacular, and maintaining strong characters in mutual respect. The two now rest solemnly next to each other and gently connect. The house has adopted an oaktree from the forest within it´s atrium. A play evolves as all the rooms surround the atrium and take part in the landscape, the forest and the ever changing seasons.

Das Haus liegt in der charakteristischen Landschaft von Tjøme, einer Insel im Oslofjord. Das bestehende kleine Landhaus stammt aus dem Jahr 1870 und ist gut erhalten. Der Kunde wünschte eine Erweiterung, die die ursprüngliche 50 m² große Hütte verdoppeln sollte. Kunde und Architekten teilten eine gemeinsame Leidenschaft für Natur und Landschaftsgestaltung. Das Grundstück befindet sich in einem dichten Laubwald, mit sanften Klippen, die aus dem Boden ragen wie der Rücken eines Wals, der aus den Wellen auftaucht. Die Architekten erkannten die Herausforderung, neue architektonische Ausdrucksformen mit der traditionellen Architektur zu verbinden und beide Identitäten in einem respektvollen Gleichgewicht zu bewahren. Jetzt stehen die beiden Gebäude harmonisch nebeneinander und sind subtil miteinander verbunden. Ein Eichenbaum aus dem Wald wurde in das Atrium des Hauses integriert. Dadurch entsteht ein Zusammenspiel, bei dem alle Räume das Atrium umgeben und Teil der Landschaft, des Waldes und des ständigen Wechsels der Jahreszeiten sind.

La maison est située dans le paysage caractéristique de Tjøme, une île du fjord d'Oslo. La petite maison de campagne existante date de 1870 et est bien conservée. Le client souhaitait une extension doublant la surface de la maison d'origine de 50 m². Client et architectes partageaient une passion commune pour la nature et le paysage. Le terrain est situé dans une forêt dense d'arbres à feuilles caduques, avec des falaises douces émergeant du sol comme le dos d'une baleine surgissant des vagues. Les architectes ont relevé le défi d'intégrer une nouvelle expression architecturale tout en respectant l'architecture vernaculaire, maintenant ainsi un équilibre harmonieux entre les deux. Désormais, les deux constructions reposent ensemble en parfaite harmonie, reliées subtilement. La maison a intégré un chêne de la forêt dans son atrium. Un jeu d'espaces est ainsi créé, où toutes les pièces s'organisent autour de l'atrium et participent au paysage, à la forêt et aux changements constants des saisons.

La casa está situada en el característico paisaje de Tjøme, una isla en el fiordo de Oslo. La pequeña casa de campo existente data de 1870 y está bien conservada. El cliente solicitó una ampliación que duplicara el tamaño de la casa original de 50 m². Cliente y arquitectos compartían una pasión común por la naturaleza y el paisajismo. El terreno está ubicado en un bosque frondoso de árboles de hoja ancha, con acantilados suaves que emergen del suelo como el lomo de una ballena surgiendo de las olas. Los arquitectos reconocieron el reto de fusionar nuevas expresiones con la arquitectura vernácula, manteniendo la identidad de ambas en un equilibrio respetuoso. Ahora, ambas construcciones reposan juntas de manera armoniosa, conectándose sutilmente. La casa ha incorporado un roble del bosque dentro de su atrio. Se genera un juego en el que todas las habitaciones rodean el atrio y participan del paisaje, el bosque y el constante cambio de las estaciones.

ARK-TELLUS

VILLA PANORAMA

VILLA PANORAMA

Akureyri, Iceland
Photos: © Alex Fradkin

The site is located in a beautiful birch forest across the water from Akureyri. In this location, it was possible to utilize spectacular views towards the town of Akureyri and see the entire fjord Eyjafjordur from north to south. With this magnificent location in mind the concept developed to having a massive and secluded lower level that carries the weight of an elevated glass house floating above. One might refer to the upper level as a tribute to Mies van der Rohe's Farnsworth house where the boundary between inside and outside are visually blurred and the entire horizon can be experienced from the house's living room.

Das Land liegt in einem schönen Birkenwald auf der anderen Seite einer Wasserzone in der Nähe der Stadt Akureyri. Auf diese Weise wurden die spektakulären Aussichten auf Akureyri und den Eyjafjordur-Fjord genutzt. Bei dieser herrlichen Lage wurde das Konzept auf der Grundlage einer isolierten unteren Ebene entwickelt, die das Gewicht eines erhöhten, schwebenden Glashauses tragen sollte. Man könnte das Obergeschoss als eine Hommage an Mies van der Rohes Farnsworth-Haus bezeichnen, in dem die Grenzen zwischen Innen und Außen visuell verschwimmen und der Horizont vom Wohnzimmer des Hauses aus erfahrbar ist.

Le terrain est situé dans une belle forêt de bouleaux de l'autre côté d'une zone d'eau près de la ville d'Akureyri. De cette façon, les vues spectaculaires d'Akureyri et du fjord de l'Eyjafjordur ont été mises à profit. Avec ce magnifique emplacement, le concept a été développé sur la base de la réalisation d'un niveau inférieur isolé qui supporterait le poids d'une maison de verre surélevée et flottante. On pourrait qualifier le niveau supérieur d'hommage à la maison Farnsworth de Mies van der Rohe, où les frontières entre l'intérieur et l'extérieur sont visuellement floues et où l'horizon peut être expérimenté depuis le salon de la maison.

El terreno está situado en un hermoso bosque de abedules al otro lado de una zona de agua cercana a la población de Akureyri. De esta forma se aprovecharon las espectaculares vistas de Akureyri y del fiordo Eyjafjordur. Con esta magnífica ubicación, el concepto se desarrolló en base a conseguir un nivel inferior aislado que soportara el peso de una casa de cristal elevada y flotante. Uno podría referirse al nivel superior como un tributo a la casa Farnsworth de Mies van der Rohe, donde los límites entre el interior y el exterior son visualmente borrosos y el horizonte puede ser experimentado desde la sala de estar de la casa.

ARKÍS ARCHITECTS

A floating glass oasis where panoramic fjord views and seamless indoor-outdoor living redefine contemporary Icelandic architecture.

VILLA BRAATHEN

VILLA BRAATHEN

Porsgrunn, Norway
Photos: © Anette Ungar, Damir Fattakhov

This home, which is located in Porsgrunn, Norway, was originally designed in a completely different way. The first draft was not approved by the municipality, and Hardy was hired to make modifications that would result in an effective approval process. This resulted in a completely new draft on the drawing board, making the total area smaller than it originally was. The building regulations required the roof to have a certain angle, and for the house to lie nicely in the terrain, a gabled roof was chosen.

Dieses Wohnhaus in Porsgrunn, Norwegen, wurde ursprünglich mit einem völlig anderen Design konzipiert. Das erste Projekt wurde von der Gemeinde nicht genehmigt, weshalb Hardy beauftragt wurde, Änderungen vorzunehmen, die die Genehmigung erleichtern würden. Dies führte zur Entwicklung eines völlig neuen Entwurfs, bei dem die Gesamtfläche im Vergleich zum ursprünglichen Projekt reduziert wurde. Die Bauvorschriften erforderten, dass das Dach eine bestimmte Neigung haben musste. Um das Haus harmonisch in das Gelände zu integrieren, entschied man sich für ein Satteldach.

Cette maison, située à Porsgrunn, en Norvège, avait été initialement conçue avec un design totalement différent. Le premier projet n'ayant pas été approuvé par la municipalité, Hardy a été engagée pour apporter des modifications facilitant son approbation. Cela a conduit à la création d'un design entièrement nouveau, réduisant la surface totale par rapport au projet initial. Les réglementations de construction imposaient un certain angle de toit, et pour que la maison s'intègre harmonieusement au terrain, un toit à deux pans a été choisi.

Esta vivienda, ubicada en Porsgrunn, Noruega, fue originalmente concebida con un diseño completamente diferente. El primer proyecto no fue aprobado por el municipio, por lo que se contrató a Hardy para realizar modificaciones que facilitaran su aprobación. Esto llevó a la creación de un diseño completamente nuevo, reduciendo el área total en comparación con el proyecto original. Las regulaciones de construcción exigían que el techo tuviera un cierto ángulo, y para que la casa se integrara adecuadamente en el terreno, se optó por un techo a dos aguas.

ARKITEKT MANUELA HARDY

VILLA MORGENSTJERNE / MORNING STAR

VILLA MORGENSTJERNE / MORNING STAR

Oslo, Norway
Photos: © Anette Ungar, Damir Fattakhov

This will be the home of a creative and musical family located just outside of downtown Oslo. The house is being built on a lot which was separated from the adjacent property and, although its design differs quite radically from the surrounding structures, it is well within the official regulation. The design of the project is born out of the architect's holistic, Scandinavian philosophy merged with the client's own interest in stylistic architecture and design. The inspiration behind the design, favoring light and spacious rooms, were in turn inspired by some of the Case Study Houses being built in Los Angeles, an architectural experiment extolling the virtues of modernist theory and industrial materials in the 1940s and 1960s.

Dies wird das Zuhause einer kreativen und musikalischen Familie am Stadtrand von Oslo. Das Haus wird auf einem abgetrennten Grundstück des Nachbargrundstücks gebaut und entspricht, obwohl es sich radikal von den umliegenden Strukturen unterscheidet, den offiziellen Bauvorschriften. Der Entwurf basiert auf der skandinavischen Philosophie der Architektin und kombiniert sie mit dem Interesse des Kunden an Architektur und stilistischem Design. Die Inspiration für das Design, das helle und großzügige Räume bevorzugt, stammt von den „Case Study Houses", die zwischen den 1940er und 1960er Jahren in Los Angeles gebaut wurden – ein architektonisches Experiment, das die Prinzipien der modernistischen Theorie und die Verwendung industrieller Materialien hervorhob.

Cette maison sera celle d'une famille créative et musicale, située en périphérie du centre d'Oslo. La construction est en cours sur un terrain détaché de la propriété voisine. Bien que son design diffère radicalement des structures environnantes, il respecte la réglementation officielle. La conception du projet s'inspire de la philosophie scandinave de l'architecte, combinée à l'intérêt du client pour l'architecture et le design stylisé. L'inspiration derrière ce design, qui privilégie des espaces vastes et lumineux, provient des « Case Study Houses » construites à Los Angeles entre les années 1940 et 1960, une expérimentation architecturale mettant en valeur les principes modernistes et l'utilisation de matériaux industriels.

Esta es la casa de una familia creativa y musical, ubicada en las afueras del centro de Oslo. La vivienda se está construyendo en un terreno segregado de la propiedad vecina y, aunque su diseño difiere radicalmente de las estructuras circundantes, cumple con la normativa oficial. El diseño del proyecto surge de la filosofía escandinava de la arquitecta, combinada con el interés del cliente por la arquitectura y el diseño estilístico. La inspiración detrás del diseño, que favorece espacios amplios y luminosos, proviene de las «Case Study Houses» construidas en Los Ángeles entre las décadas de 1940 y 1960, un experimento arquitectónico que exaltaba las virtudes de la teoría modernista y el uso de materiales industriales.

ARKITEKT MANUELA HARDY

SKRIVESTUE FALDBAKKEN

SKRIVESTUE FALDBAKKEN

Hamar, Norway
Photos: © asas arkitektur as

The Skrivestue Faldbakken is situated in the rural areas outside the city of Hamar. The big site has a great view overlooking the fields dancing down towards Norway's largest lake Mjøsa, and consists of several linked houses from different eras. The client is the well known author Knut Faldbakken and his wife Kirvil. The new extension of the house is designed to link the different existing buildings. It is planned as a contemporary wooden building designed to emphasize outward views and the use of natural light. Old and new houses meet with mutual respect to one another, both indoors and outdoors. The function of the 20 m^2 house is triple; writing room, family room and winter garden. Shapes and materiality of the box follows and respects the existing buildings, and the transitions are emphasized as recessions in the facade. The construction is made of CLT and the cladding is spruce treated with iron sulphate.

Skrivestue Faldbakken befindet sich in einer ländlichen Gegend am Stadtrand von Hamar. Das weitläufige Grundstück bietet einen beeindruckenden Blick auf die Felder, die zum Mjøsa-See hin abfallen – dem größten See Norwegens – und besteht aus mehreren miteinander verbundenen Häusern aus verschiedenen Epochen. Die Bauherren sind der bekannte Autor Knut Faldbakken und seine Frau Kirvil. Der neue Anbau des Hauses wurde entworfen, um die verschiedenen bestehenden Gebäude zu verbinden. Es handelt sich um eine moderne Holzkonstruktion, die die Aussicht nach außen und die Nutzung des natürlichen Lichts betont. Alt und neu begegnen sich mit gegenseitigem Respekt, sowohl im Inneren als auch im Äußeren. Der 20 m^2 große Neubau erfüllt drei Funktionen: Schreibzimmer, Familienraum und Gewächshaus. Die Form und Materialität der Struktur folgen und respektieren die bestehenden Gebäude, mit Übergängen, die sich als Rücksprünge in der Fassade abzeichnen. Die Konstruktion besteht aus CLT, und die Außenverkleidung ist aus mit Eisensulfat behandelter Fichte gefertigt.

Skrivestue Faldbakken est située dans une zone rurale en périphérie de la ville de Hamar. Le vaste terrain offre une vue imprenable sur les champs qui descendent vers le lac Mjøsa, le plus grand de Norvège, et se compose de plusieurs maisons interconnectées de différentes époques. Les clients sont l'écrivain renommé Knut Faldbakken et son épouse Kirvil. La nouvelle extension de la maison a été conçue pour relier les différents bâtiments existants. Elle se présente comme une construction contemporaine en bois qui met en valeur les vues extérieures et l'exploitation de la lumière naturelle. Les maisons anciennes et nouvelles se rencontrent dans un respect mutuel, tant à l'intérieur qu'à l'extérieur. La nouvelle construction de 20 m^2 remplit trois fonctions : bureau d'écriture, salon familial et serre. La forme et la matérialité de la structure suivent et respectent les bâtiments existants, avec des transitions marquées par des retraits dans la façade. La construction est réalisée en CLT et le revêtement est en épicéa traité au sulfate de fer.

Skrivestue Faldbakken está situada en una zona rural a las afueras de la ciudad de Hamar. El extenso terreno ofrece una vista impresionante de los campos que descienden hacia el lago Mjøsa, el más grande de Noruega, y está compuesto por varias casas interconectadas de diferentes épocas. Los clientes son el reconocido autor Knut Faldbakken y su esposa Kirvil. La nueva ampliación de la casa ha sido diseñada para conectar los distintos edificios existentes. Se concibe como una construcción contemporánea de madera que enfatiza las vistas al exterior y el aprovechamiento de la luz natural. Las casas antiguas y nuevas se encuentran con un respeto mutuo, tanto en el interior como en el exterior. La nueva construcción de 20 m^2 cumple tres funciones: sala de escritura, sala familiar e invernadero. La forma y materialidad de la estructura siguen y respetan los edificios existentes, con transiciones que se destacan como retranqueos en la fachada. La construcción está hecha de CLT y el revestimiento es de abeto tratado con sulfato de hierro.

ASAS ARKITEKTUR

Nestled in the Norwegian countryside, this extension blends past and present, embracing light and landscape with precision.

TONEHEIM FOLKEHØGSKOLE – STUDENT HOUSING

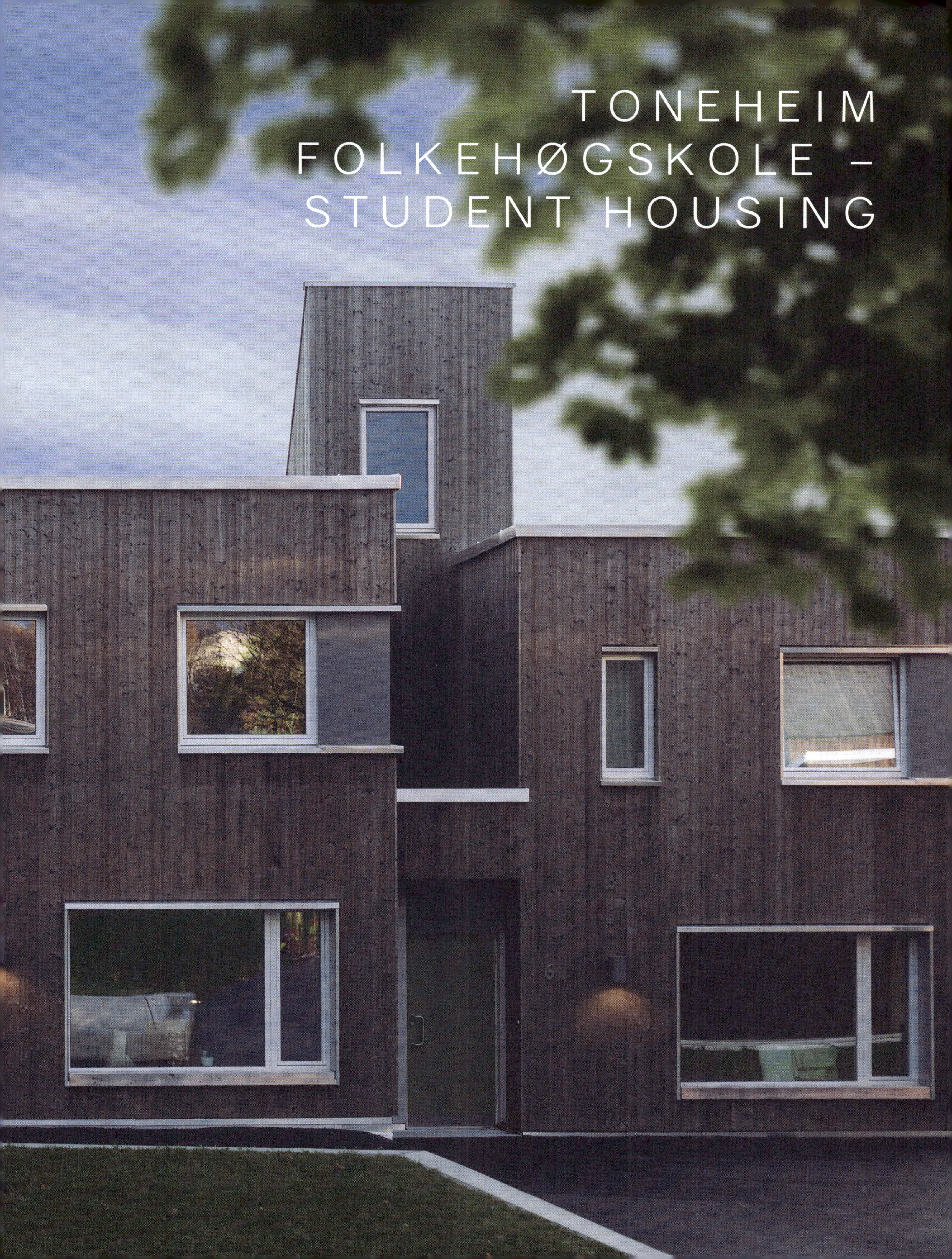

TONEHEIM FOLKEHØGSKOLE – STUDENT HOUSING

Innlandet, Norway
Photos: © asas arkitektur as, Fredrik Myhre, Ola Spangen

The project contains new student housing at Toneheim Folkehøgskole in the county of Innlandet, Norway. The project is organized around a common yard, a Norwegian traditional typology called "tun", a place where traditions meets modern architecture with a personal expression. Toneheim is designed according to the passive house standard with a compact plan and a chained building structure with smaller facades and thus a limited loss of heat from the building blocks. The stairwells functions as environmental towers bringing day light to the core, sends unwanted surplus heat out of the building and has sun catchers facing south, for water heating. This roof tower landscape connects to the tower at Vang church as the local context and emphasizes a vernacular architectural feature with multiple functions.

Das Projekt umfasst neue Studentenwohnungen für die Toneheim Folkehøgskole im norwegischen Landkreis Innlandet. Die Organisation des Projekts orientiert sich an einem gemeinsamen Innenhof, basierend auf einer traditionellen norwegischen Typologie namens „tun", in der Tradition und moderne Architektur in einem persönlichen Ausdruck aufeinandertreffen. Toneheim wurde nach Passivhaus-Standards entworfen, mit einer kompakten Anordnung und einer aneinandergereihten Gebäudestruktur mit kleineren Fassaden, um Wärmeverluste zu minimieren. Die Treppen fungieren als klimatische Türme, die natürliches Licht in den Gebäudekern leiten, überschüssige Wärme abführen und Sonnenenergie aus dem Süden für die Warmwasserbereitung nutzen. Diese Dachlandschaft mit Türmen verbindet sich mit dem Kirchturm von Vang und integriert sich in den lokalen Kontext, während sie gleichzeitig ein architektonisches Merkmal mit mehreren Funktionen hervorhebt.

Le projet concerne de nouveaux logements pour étudiants à l'école Toneheim Folkehøgskole, dans le comté d'Innlandet, en Norvège. L'organisation du projet s'articule autour d'une cour commune, suivant une typologie norvégienne traditionnelle appelée « tun », où la tradition rencontre l'architecture moderne dans une expression personnelle. Toneheim a été conçu selon les standards des maisons passives, avec une distribution compacte et une structure en enfilade de bâtiments aux façades plus petites, réduisant ainsi les pertes de chaleur. Les escaliers servent de tours climatiques, apportant de la lumière naturelle au cœur du bâtiment, évacuant l'excès de chaleur et captant la lumière du soleil depuis le sud pour chauffer l'eau. Ce paysage de tours sur les toits s'intègre avec le clocher de l'église de Vang, créant un lien avec le contexte local et mettant en valeur un trait architectural vernaculaire aux multiples fonctions.

El proyecto consiste en nuevas viviendas para estudiantes en la escuela Toneheim Folkehøgskole, en el condado de Innlandet, Noruega. La organización del proyecto gira en torno a un patio común, siguiendo una tipología tradicional noruega llamada «tun», donde la tradición se encuentra con la arquitectura moderna en una expresión personal. Toneheim ha sido diseñado según los estándares de casa pasiva, con una distribución compacta y una estructura encadenada de edificios con fachadas más pequeñas, lo que reduce la pérdida de calor. Las escaleras funcionan como torres ambientales, proporcionando luz natural al núcleo del edificio, expulsando el calor excedente y captando la luz solar desde el sur para calentar agua. Este paisaje de torres en los tejados se conecta con la torre de la iglesia de Vang, integrándose en el contexto local y destacando un rasgo arquitectónico vernáculo con múltiples funciones.

ASAS ARKITEKTUR

LUNDNÄS HOUSE

LUNDNÄS HOUSE

Hälsingland, Sweden
Photos: © Johan Sellén

The Lundnäs House is built in the granite foundation from a turn of the century ceramic stove factory. The architect designed and built the house as a case stucy with design and construction evolving simultaneously using experimental ideas, such as a floor that is heated by hot air from the fireplace and passive solar heating. The secluded location and scenery made it desirable to have glass walls around the living area while the bedrooms and bathroom are located in the back of the house between walls built of granite and bricks recovered from the site. The house is an example of how thoughtful construction, using locally produced materials, and taking into account the nature and history of the region can combine contemporary aesthetics and philosophy with functional requirements, low construction costs, and a small ecological footprint.

Das Lundnäs-Haus ist im Granitfundament einer Keramikofenfabrik aus der Jahrhundertwende erbaut. Der Architekt entwarf und baute das Haus als Fallstudie, wobei sich Entwurf und Konstruktion gleichzeitig mit experimentellen Ideen weiterentwickelten, wie beispielsweise ein Fußboden, der durch heiße Luft aus dem Kamin und passive Solarheizung beheizt wird. Aufgrund der abgeschiedenen Lage und Landschaft war es wünschenswert, den Wohnbereich mit Glaswänden zu umgeben, während sich die Schlafzimmer und das Badezimmer im hinteren Teil des Hauses zwischen Wänden aus Granit und Ziegelsteinen befinden, die vor der Baustelle verborgen wurden. Das Haus ist ein Beispiel dafür, wie durchdachtes Bauen unter Verwendung lokal produzierter Materialien und unter Berücksichtigung der Natur und Geschichte der Region zeitgenössische Ästhetik und Philosophie mit funktionalen Anforderungen, niedrigen Baukosten und einem kleinen ökologischen Fußabdruck verbinden kann.

La maison Lundnäs est construite dans les fondations en granit d'une usine de poêles en céramique du tournant du siècle. L'architecte a conçu et construit la maison comme une étude de cas ; la conception et la construction évoluant simultanément grâce à des idées expérimentales, comme un plancher chauffé par l'air chaud de la cheminée et le chauffage solaire passif. L'emplacement et le paysage isolés ont rendu souhaitable la présence de murs en verre autour de la zone de séjour, tandis que les chambres et la salle de bain sont situées à l'arrière de la maison entre des murs construits en granit et en briques récupérées sur le site. La maison est un exemple de la manière dont une construction réfléchie, utilisant des matériaux produits localement et tenant compte de la nature et de l'histoire de la région, peut combiner l'esthétique et la philosophie contemporaines avec des exigences fonctionnelles, de faibles coûts de construction et une faible empreinte écologique.

La casa Lundnäs está construida en los cimientos de granito de una fábrica de estufas de cerámica de principios de siglo. El arquitecto diseñó y construyó la casa como un caso de estudio, donde el diseño y la construcción evolucionan simultáneamente usando ideas experimentales, como un suelo que se calienta con el aire caliente de la chimenea y la calefacción solar pasiva. La ubicación aislada y el paisaje hicieron que fuera deseable tener paredes de vidrio alrededor de la zona de estar, mientras que los dormitorios y el baño se encuentran en la parte trasera de la casa entre paredes construidas de granito y ladrillos recuperados del lugar. La casa es un ejemplo de cómo una construcción cuidadosa, utilizando materiales producidos localmente y teniendo en cuenta la naturaleza y la historia de la región, puede combinar la estética y la filosofía contemporáneas con requisitos funcionales, bajos costos de construcción y una pequeña huella ecológica.

DELIN ARKITEKTKONTOR

Built atop a historic foundation, Lundnäs House merges experimental heating techniques, reclaimed materials, and panoramic glass walls for a truly sustainable retreat.

I/O CABIN

I/O CABIN

Risør, Norway
Photos: © Carlos Rollán

Three separate volumes are connected by a wooden deck floating above the sloped terrain of solid rock. Under a shared, cantilevered roof, the atrium shaped floor plan creates an "inside/outside" effect for its purpose as a summer house - using the outdoor spaces as much as the indoors. The summer cabin is wrapped in locally sourced spruce siding, impregnated with an organic wood protection with gray color pigments. The interior walls are all out of white painted, horizontal wood siding that meets a warmer toned floor and ceiling of white oiled spruce - typical to traditional and older cabins on the coast of Norway. The wooden pillars lifting the cabin off the ground are connected with cross-laminated timber beams in the deck, continuing all the way up to the roof construction which copies the structural beams in the deck. A V-shaped wood column caries the weight of the cantilevered roof as a large glass corner opens the main living space to its surrounding natural elements.

Drei separate Volumina sind durch eine Plattform aus Holz verbunden, die über dem geneigten Gelände aus festem Fels schwebt. Unter einem gemeinsamen überhängenden Dach erzeugt der atriumförmige Grundriss einen „drinnen/draußen"-Effekt für die Nutzung als Sommerhaus, wobei die äußeren Räume ebenso wie die inneren genutzt werden. Die Sommerhütte ist in einheimische Fichte gehüllt, die mit einem organischen Holzschutzmittel mit grauen Farbpigmenten imprägniert ist. Die Innenwände sind alle aus weiß gestrichener Holzverkleidung gefertigt, die auf einen wärmeren Ton von geölter weißer Fichte trifft, typisch für traditionelle und alte Hütten an der norwegischen Küste. Die Holzpfosten, die die Hütte vom Boden abheben, sind mit Brettschichtholzbalken auf der Plattform verbunden, die sich bis zur Dachstruktur fortsetzen, die die strukturellen Balken auf der Plattform kopiert. Eine V-förmige Holzsäule trägt das Gewicht des überhängenden Daches, während ein großes Fenster den Hauptwohnbereich zu seinen umgebenden natürlichen Elementen öffnet.

Trois volumes séparés sont reliés par une plateforme en bois flottant sur le terrain incliné de roche solide. Sous un toit en porte-à-faux partagé, le plan d'étage en forme d'atrium crée un effet « intérieur/extérieur » pour une utilisation en tant que maison d'été, utilisant les espaces extérieurs autant que les intérieurs. La cabane d'été est enveloppée de sapin d'origine locale, imprégné d'une protection organique pour le bois avec des pigments de couleur grise. Les murs intérieurs sont tous en lambris de bois peint en blanc, qui rencontre un sol et un plafond de teinte plus chaude en sapin blanc huilé, typique des cabanes traditionnelles et anciennes de la côte norvégienne. Les piliers en bois surélevant la cabine du sol sont reliés par des poutres en bois lamellé-collé sur la plateforme, se poursuivant jusqu'à la structure du toit qui reproduit les poutres structurales sur la plateforme. Une colonne de bois en forme de V supporte le poids du toit en porte-à-faux tandis qu'une grande baie vitrée ouvre l'espace de vie principal à ses éléments naturels environnants.

Tres volúmenes separados quedan conectados por una plataforma de madera que flota sobre el terreno inclinado de roca sólida. Bajo un techo compartido en voladizo, el plano de planta en forma de atrio crea un efecto «dentro/fuera» para su uso como casa de verano. La cabaña de verano está envuelta de abeto de origen local, impregnado con una protección orgánica para madera con pigmentos de color gris. Las paredes interiores están todas hechas de revestimiento de madera pintada de blanco, que se encuentra con un suelo y techo de tono más cálido de abeto blanco aceitado, típico de cabañas tradicionales de la costa Noruega. Los pilares de madera que elevan la cabaña del suelo están conectados con vigas de madera contralaminada en la plataforma, continuando hasta la estructura del techo que copia las vigas estructurales en la plataforma. Una columna de madera en forma de V soporta el peso del techo en voladizo mientras que un gran ventanal abre el espacio de estar principal a sus elementos naturales circundantes.

ERLING BERG

Floating above rugged terrain, this summer retreat balances Norwegian tradition with mid-century influences, seamlessly blending architecture and nature under a cantilevered roof.

MYLLA
WINTER CABIN

MYLLA WINTER CABIN

Oslo, Norway
Photos: © Einar Aslaksen

Nestled in Nordmarka, north of Oslo, Mylla Cabin harmonizes with nature through a simple, functional design. Built with pine wood treated using the Norwegian "Møre Royal" technique, its exterior ages naturally, blending with the landscape. Inside, varnished spruce and polished concrete create a warm, durable atmosphere. Designed to near passive house standards, it relies solely on geothermal energy for heating. Its elongated layout separates bedrooms from communal areas, with large windows framing the surrounding scenery. The staircase, a central design element, connects levels and shapes the spatial composition.

In Nordmarka, nördlich von Oslo gelegen, fügt sich Mylla Cabin mit einem schlichten, funktionalen Design in die Natur ein. Die Außenverkleidung aus Kiefernholz, behandelt mit der norwegischen „Møre Royal"-Technik, entwickelt mit der Zeit eine natürliche Patina. Innen sorgen lackierte Fichte und polierter Beton für eine warme, robuste Atmosphäre. Nach nahezu Passivhaus-Standards gebaut, wird sie ausschließlich mit Erdwärme beheizt. Die langgestreckte Raumaufteilung trennt Schlafbereiche von Gemeinschaftsräumen, große Fenster rahmen die Landschaft. Die Treppe, ein zentrales Designelement, verbindet Ebenen und prägt die räumliche Struktur.

Située à Nordmarka, au nord d'Oslo, Mylla Cabin s'intègre harmonieusement à la nature avec un design simple et fonctionnel. Construite en pin traité selon la technique norvégienne « Møre Royal », son extérieur vieillit naturellement et se fond dans le paysage. À l'intérieur, l'épicéa verni et le béton poli créent une ambiance chaleureuse et résistante. Conçue selon des normes proches de la maison passive, elle est exclusivement chauffée par énergie géothermique. Son agencement allongé sépare chambres et espaces communs, avec de grandes fenêtres encadrant le paysage. L'escalier, élément clé du design, relie les niveaux et structure l'espace.

Ubicada en Nordmarka, un bosque al norte de Oslo, Mylla Cabin respeta la naturaleza con un diseño simple y funcional. Construida con madera de pino tratada con el método noruego «Møre Royal», su exterior envejece con el entorno, desarrollando una pátina natural. En el interior, abeto barnizado y hormigón pulido generan una atmósfera cálida y resistente. Con estándares de casa pasiva, se calienta exclusivamente con energía geotérmica. Su distribución alargada separa dormitorios y zonas comunes, con grandes ventanales que enmarcan el paisaje. La escalera, pieza clave del diseño, une niveles y define la estructura espacial.

FJORD ARKITEKTER

Mylla Cabin blends tradition and innovation, using sustainable materials and geothermal energy to create a timeless retreat in the Norwegian wilderness.

CABIN EILEVSTØLEN

CABIN EILEVSTØLEN

Geilo, Norway
Photos: © Isaac Voelcker, GOA Arkitektkontor

An isolated cabin retreat located in the open landscape surrounding Geilo, Norway. The project comprises two buildings: the main cabin and the guesthouse. The main cabin features a traditional program of three bedrooms and generous open-plan living space, all facing the spectacular view of the surrounding mountains. The guesthouse is compact and efficient in its planning, but is afforded a rich hierarchy of spaces despite its miniature footprint. The project reframes the traditional cabin typology within a contemporary architectural expression, while using form and volume to explore the gradation from enclosure to the open landscape. Rigorous yet simple detailing is applied throughout, giving both interior and exterior a sense of calm resolution.

Ein abgeschiedenes Hüttenrefugium in der offenen Landschaft von Geilo, Norwegen. Das Projekt besteht aus zwei Gebäuden: der Haupthütte und dem Gästehaus. Die Haupthütte folgt einem traditionellen Schema mit drei Schlafzimmern und einem großzügigen offenen Wohnbereich, der sich zu den spektakulären Ausblicken auf die umliegenden Berge hin orientiert. Das Gästehaus, obwohl kompakt und effizient in seiner Aufteilung, bietet eine reiche Raumhierarchie trotz seiner geringen Größe. Das Projekt interpretiert die traditionelle Hüttentypologie in einer zeitgenössischen architektonischen Ausdrucksweise neu, indem es Form und Volumen nutzt, um den Übergang vom geschützten Innenraum zur offenen Landschaft zu erforschen. Sorgfältige, aber einfache Details werden im gesamten Design angewendet, um sowohl innen als auch außen eine ruhige Atmosphäre zu schaffen.

Un refuge de cabanes isolées dans le paysage ouvert de Geilo, en Norvège. Le projet comprend deux bâtiments : la cabane principale et la maison d'amis. La cabane principale suit un schéma traditionnel avec trois chambres et un vaste espace de vie ouvert, orienté vers les vues spectaculaires sur les montagnes environnantes. La maison d'amis, bien que compacte et efficace dans sa distribution, offre une hiérarchie d'espaces riche malgré sa petite taille. Le projet réinterprète la typologie traditionnelle de la cabane dans une expression architecturale contemporaine, en utilisant la forme et le volume pour explorer la transition entre l'abri et le paysage ouvert. Des détails rigoureux mais simples sont appliqués tout au long du design, procurant une sensation de calme tant à l'intérieur qu'à l'extérieur.

Un refugio de cabañas aisladas en el paisaje abierto de Geilo, Noruega. El proyecto consta de dos edificios: la cabaña principal y la casa de huéspedes. La cabaña principal sigue un esquema tradicional con tres dormitorios y una generosa área de estar de planta abierta, orientada hacia las espectaculares vistas de las montañas circundantes. La casa de huéspedes, aunque compacta y eficiente en su distribución, ofrece una jerarquía de espacios rica a pesar de su reducido tamaño. El proyecto replantea la tipología tradicional de la cabaña dentro de una expresión arquitectónica contemporánea, utilizando forma y volumen para explorar la transición del refugio al paisaje abierto. Se aplican detalles rigurosos pero sencillos en todo el diseño, proporcionando una sensación de calma tanto en el interior como en el exterior.

GOA ARKITEKTKONTOR

Set against Norway's vast mountain landscape, this retreat reinterprets traditional cabin design with refined details and a seamless connection to nature.

PRIVATE HOUSE, KIRKEVEIEN

PRIVATE HOUSE, KIRKEVEIEN

Oslo, Norway
Photos: © Isaac Voelcker, GOA Arkitektkontor

Three storey house situated in outer Oslo. Despite its compact plan, the design meets the client's aspirations for a single, open-plan living space occupying the entire second floor, and dramatic roof terrace affording glimpses of the Oslo fjord. The essence of the brief was to maximise natural light and a sense of generous openness without compromising the need for privacy from adjacent properties. These considerations drive the design and detailing of the external envelope - essentially a series of timber curtains - giving the building its characteristic external expression while also serving practical functions such as protection from falling.

Ein dreigeschossiges Haus am Stadtrand von Oslo. Trotz seiner kompakten Aufteilung erfüllt das Design die Wünsche des Bauherrn nach einem einzigen offenen Wohnbereich, der das gesamte zweite Geschoss einnimmt, sowie nach einer spektakulären Dachterrasse mit Blick auf den Oslofjord. Der Kern des Entwurfs bestand darin, maximales natürliches Licht und ein großzügiges Raumgefühl zu schaffen, ohne die Privatsphäre gegenüber den Nachbargrundstücken zu beeinträchtigen. Diese Überlegungen bestimmten das Design und die Details der Außenhülle, die aus einer Reihe von hölzernen „Vorhängen" besteht. Diese verleihen dem Gebäude seine charakteristische Ausdrucksweise und erfüllen gleichzeitig praktische Funktionen wie den Absturzschutz.

Maison de trois étages située en périphérie d'Oslo. Malgré une distribution compacte, le design répond aux aspirations du client en offrant un espace de vie ouvert occupant tout le deuxième étage, ainsi qu'une spectaculaire terrasse sur le toit avec vue sur le fjord d'Oslo. L'essence du projet était de maximiser la lumière naturelle et la sensation d'espace sans compromettre l'intimité par rapport aux propriétés voisines. Ces considérations ont guidé la conception et les détails de l'enveloppe extérieure, qui se compose d'une série de « rideaux » en bois conférant au bâtiment son expression caractéristique, tout en remplissant des fonctions pratiques telles que la protection contre les chutes.

Casa de tres plantas situada en las afueras de Oslo. A pesar de su distribución compacta, el diseño cumple con las aspiraciones del cliente de contar con un único espacio de estar de planta abierta que ocupe todo el segundo piso, además de una espectacular terraza en la azotea con vistas al fiordo de Oslo. La esencia del encargo era maximizar la luz natural y la sensación de amplitud sin comprometer la privacidad respecto a las propiedades vecinas. Estas consideraciones impulsaron el diseño y los detalles de la envolvente exterior, que consiste en una serie de «cortinas» de madera que le otorgan a la construcción su expresión característica, al tiempo que cumplen funciones prácticas como la protección contra caídas.

GOA ARKITEKTKONTOR

Timber curtains shape this Oslo home, balancing openness and privacy while framing fjord views and maximizing natural light across three levels.

VACATION-RESIDENCE EAGLES DREAM

VACATION-RESIDENCE EAGLES DREAM

Stykkishólmur, Iceland
Photos: © Gunnar Sverrisson

Suspended above Iceland's untamed terrain, Eagles Dream merges architecture and landscape. Inspired by an eagle feather, the house stands on columns, preserving nature below. With breathtaking views in every direction, its design emphasizes lightness. The Kebony Clear wood and Alucoil panels continue under the structure, ensuring material unity. Inside, Icelandic Bluestone and veneer-clad pine complement the natural surroundings. The corridor features floor windows connecting to the earth, while trapezoidal shapes in the library and kitchen mimic vintage camera lenses, framing the stunning scenery.

Hoch über der isländischen Landschaft thront Eagles Dream und verbindet Architektur mit Natur. Inspiriert von einer Adlerfeder, ruht das Haus auf Säulen und bewahrt die unberührte Umgebung. Mit atemberaubenden Ausblicken in alle Richtungen betont das Design Leichtigkeit. Kebony Clear-Holz und Alucoil-Paneele setzen sich unter der Struktur fort, um Materialkontinuität zu gewährleisten. Im Inneren schaffen isländischer Blaustein und furniertes Kiefernholz eine harmonische Verbindung zur Natur. Bodentiefe Fenster im Korridor stellen eine Verbindung zur Erde her, während trapezförmige Elemente in Bibliothek und Küche an alte Kameralinsen erinnern und die Landschaft einrahmen.

Suspendue au-dessus du paysage islandais, Eagles Dream fusionne architecture et nature. Inspirée par une plume d'aigle, la maison repose sur des colonnes, préservant l'environnement en dessous. Offrant des vues spectaculaires dans toutes les directions, son design privilégie la légèreté. Le bois Kebony Clear et les panneaux Alucoil se prolongent sous la structure, assurant une continuité matérielle. À l'intérieur, la pierre bleue islandaise et le pin plaqué renforcent l'harmonie avec la nature. Des fenêtres au sol relient le corridor à la terre, tandis que les formes trapézoïdales de la bibliothèque et de la cuisine évoquent des objectifs de caméra anciens, capturant la beauté du paysage.

Elevado sobre la naturaleza islandesa, Eagles Dream fusiona arquitectura y paisaje. Inspirada en una pluma de águila, la casa se alza sobre columnas para preservar el entorno. Con vistas espectaculares en todas direcciones, su diseño enfatiza la ligereza. La madera Kebony Clear y los paneles Alucoil se extienden bajo la estructura para garantizar unidad material. En el interior, la piedra azul islandesa y el pino enchapado refuerzan la conexión con el paisaje. Ventanas en el suelo del corredor vinculan con la tierra, mientras que formas trapezoidales en la biblioteca y cocina evocan lentes de cámara antiguas, enmarcando la naturaleza.

GUDMUNDUR JONSSON ARKITEKTKONTOR

CASA MYHRER HAUGE

CASA MYHRER HAUGE

Oslo, Norway
Photos: © Jiri Havran

The concept of Casa Myhrer Hauge is a synthesis of bringing difficult landscape and regulation factors together. The factors being a river down the valley on the s-vest side of the site, with prohibitions to build closer than 100 meters, and the partly closed river/stream, that I found important to open up, make use of, preserve the nature, and bring the stream into the project as an important feature.
Due to those issues, and the wish to enhance the importance between the stream and the project, the garage and the house are connected with a bridge floating over the landscape, not touching it, but bringing it into importance and meditative experience when entering the house. The nature will be brought back as natural as possible, as it was initially in this Maridalen forest, just enhancing the nature with simple means, with the treatment of the Stream.

Das Konzept der Casa Myhrer Hauge ist eine Synthese aus der Zusammenführung von schwierigem Gelände und Vorschriften. Ein talabwärts verlaufender Fluss auf der Südseite des Geländes, mit Bauverboten näher als 100 Meter, und der teilweise geschlossene Flusslauf, den der Architekt für wichtig erachtete, unter Wahrung der Natur zu erschließen und den Bach in das Projekt einzubringen, waren die wichtigsten Merkmale.
Aus diesen Gründen und aus dem Wunsch heraus, die Bedeutung zwischen dem Bach und dem Projekt zu erhöhen, sind die Garage und das Haus mit einer schwimmenden Brücke verbunden, die das Betreten des Gebäudes in eine meditative Erfahrung verwandelt. Die Natur wird so natürlich wie möglich zurückgebracht, so wie sie in diesem Maridalen-Wald ursprünglich war.

Le concept de la Casa Myhrer Hauge est une synthèse entre un paysage difficile et des réglementations. Parmi les éléments les plus importants on trouve une rivière descendant la vallée sur le côté sud du site, avec des interdictions de construire à moins de 100 m et le cours d'eau partiellement fermé, que l'architecte a jugé important d'ouvrir tout en préservant la nature et d'intégrer le cours d'eau dans le projet.
En raison de ces problèmes et du souhait d'accroître l'importance entre le ruisseau et le projet, le garage et la maison sont reliés par un pont flottant, ce qui permet de vivre une expérience méditative en entrant dans le bâtiment. La nature sera ramenée aussi naturelle que possible, comme elle l'était initialement dans cette forêt de Maridalen.

La Casa Myhrer Hauge es el resultado de unir un entorno complicado y las regulaciones legales: la presencia de un río en el lado sur del terreno, las prohibiciones de construir a menos de 100 m, y un arroyo que el arquitecto consideró importante ampliar preservando la naturaleza.
Debido a esas cuestiones y al deseo de resaltar la importancia del arroyo en el proyecto, el garaje y la casa se conectaron por medio de un puente flotante, convirtiendo la intervención en una experiencia meditativa durante la entrada al edificio. La naturaleza se recupera de la manera más natural posible, tal como ya sucedió originalmente en este bosque de Maridalen.

GUDMUNDUR JONSSON ARKITEKTKONTOR

BIRKEDAL

BIRKEDAL

Møn, Denmark
Photos: © Jesper Ray, Lene K Fotografi

"Birkedal", or "Birch Dale" in English, was designed and built single handily by Jan Henrik Jansen with the goal to create a sustainable and peaceful family retreat on the bucolic Danish island of Møn. The house comprises nine interlinked cylindrical volumes constructed with intricate timber frames and clad with narrow spruce trunks which are a waste product of the forestry industry. Each of the cylinders encloses a single idiosyncratic room, finished with richly textured white surfaces; river pebble floors and painted board and batten wall cladding, which, like the walls of a gallery, provide a calm backdrop for the constantly changing textures and colours of the agricultural landscape visible through the punctured rectangular windows. The unique layout of the house demanded specially designed furniture, materials and details throughout.

Birkedal, oder auf Deutsch „Birkental", wurde von Jan Henrik Jansen eigenhändig entworfen und gebaut, mit dem Ziel, ein nachhaltiges und friedliches Familienrefugium auf der bukolischen dänischen Insel Møn zu schaffen. Das Haus besteht aus neun miteinander verbundenen zylindrischen Volumina, die mit komplizierten Holzrahmen gebaut und mit schmalen Fichtenstämmen verkleidet wurden, die ein Abfallprodukt der Forstwirtschaft sind. Jeder der Zylinder umschließt einen einzelnen, eigenwilligen Raum, der mit reich strukturierten, weißen Oberflächen versehen ist; Böden aus Flusskieselsteinen und Wandverkleidungen aus gestrichenen Brettern und Latten, die wie die Wände einer Galerie einen ruhigen Hintergrund für die ständig wechselnden Texturen und Farben der Agrarlandschaft bilden, die durch die durchbrochenen rechteckigen Fenster sichtbar sind. Der einzigartige Grundriss des Hauses erforderte durchgehend speziell entworfene Möbel, Materialien und Details.

« Birkedal », ou « Vallée des bouleaux » en français, a été conçu et construite à la main par Jan Henrik Jansen dans le but de créer une retraite familiale durable et paisible sur la bucolique île danoise de Møn. La maison se compose de neuf volumes cylindriques reliés entre eux, construits avec des charpentes en bois complexes et habillés d'étroites branches d'épicéa qui sont un déchet de l'industrie forestière. Chacun des cylindres renferme une pièce unique, avec des surfaces blanches richement texturées, des sols en galets de rivière et un revêtement mural en planches et lattes peintes. Cela offre, au même titre que les murs d'une galerie, une toile de fond calme aux textures et couleurs en constante évolution du paysage agricole, visible à travers les fenêtres rectangulaires percées. L'agencement unique de la maison exigeait des meubles, des matériaux et des détails spécialement conçus pour l'ensemble de la maison.

«Birkedal», «Valle del Abedul» en español, fue diseñado y construido a mano por Jan Henrik Jansen con el objetivo de crear un refugio familiar sostenible y pacífico en la bucólica isla danesa de Møn. La casa comprende nueve volúmenes cilíndricos entrelazados, construidos con intrincados marcos de madera y revestidos con estrechas ramas de abeto que son un producto de desecho de la industria forestal. Cada uno de los cilindros encierra una única habitación acabada con superficies blancas de rica textura; suelos de guijarros de río y revestimientos de tablas y listones pintados, que, como las paredes de una galería, proporcionan un tranquilo telón de fondo para las texturas y colores constantemente cambiantes del paisaje agrícola visible a través de las ventanas rectangulares perforadas. La disposición única de la casa exigía muebles, materiales y detalles especialmente diseñados.

JAN HENRIK JANSEN ARKITEKTER

Nine interlinked cylinders form this serene Danish retreat, where natural materials and bespoke details create a dialogue with the surrounding landscape.

VILLA KORUP

VILLA KORUP

Fyn, Denmark
Photos: © Gabrielle Gualdi, Marshall Blecher

Villa Korup was designed for a young family of six on the Danish island of Fyn. The characteristic "three legged" plan was developed in order to delineate the different aspects of the landscape, accentuating their qualities and creating three characteristic courtyard like spaces; a sunny south facing sloped area to the south, a protected kitchen garden to the east and an orchard cum playground to the west. Internally, the plan provides central communal spaces for the large family to gather as well as more private, secluded spaces at the ends of the wings. The house is constructed entirely from cross laminated timber (CLT) and clad with panels of weathering steel which change tone and respond to the sites conditions. Villa Korup was designed in collaboration with Australian architect Marshall Blecher.

Die Villa Korup wurde für eine junge sechsköpfige Familie auf der dänischen Insel Fünen entworfen. Der charakteristische „dreibeinige" Grundriss wurde entwickelt, um die verschiedenen Aspekte der Landschaft abzugrenzen, ihre Qualitäten hervorzuheben und drei charakteristische hofähnliche Räume zu schaffen: einen sonnigen, nach Süden ausgerichteten Hang, einen geschützten Nutzgarten im Osten und einen Obstgarten mit Spielplatz im Westen. Im Inneren sieht der Plan zentrale Gemeinschaftsräume vor, in denen sich die große Familie versammeln kann, sowie privatere, abgelegene Räume an den Enden der Flügel. Das Haus ist vollständig aus Brettsperrholz (CLT) gebaut und mit Paneelen aus verwitterndem Stahl verkleidet, die ihren Farbton ändern und auf die Bedingungen des Standortes reagieren. Die Villa Korup wurde in Zusammenarbeit mit dem australischen Architekten Marshall Blecher entworfen.

La Villa Korup a été conçue pour une jeune famille de six personnes sur l'île danoise de Fyn. Le plan caractéristique « à trois pattes » a été élaboré afin de délimiter les différents aspects du paysage, en accentuant leurs qualités et en créant trois espaces caractéristiques ressemblant à des cours. Il s'agit d'une zone en pente ensoleillée orientée au sud, d'un potager protégé à l'est et d'un verger et une aire de jeu à l'ouest. À l'intérieur, le plan prévoit des espaces communs centraux pour que la grande famille puisse se réunir, ainsi que des espaces plus privés et isolés aux extrémités des ailes. La maison est entièrement construite en bois lamellé-collé croisé (CLT) et revêtue de panneaux d'acier résistants aux intempéries qui changent de ton et réagissent aux conditions du site. La Villa Korup a été conçue en collaboration avec l'architecte australien Marshall Blecher.

Villa Korup fue diseñada para una joven familia de seis miembros en la isla danesa de Fyn. El característico plan de «tres patas» se desarrolló para delinear los diferentes aspectos del paisaje, acentuando sus cualidades y creando tres espacios característicos a modo de patio; una zona soleada orientada al sur con pendiente al sur, un jardín con cocina exterior protegido al este y un huerto con patio de recreo al oeste. Internamente, el plan prevé espacios comunitarios centrales para que se reúna la familia numerosa, así como espacios más privados y aislados en los extremos de las alas. La casa está construida enteramente de madera laminada en cruz (CLT) y revestida con paneles de acero resistente a la intemperie que cambian de tono y responden a las condiciones del lugar. Villa Korup fue diseñada en colaboración con el arquitecto australiano Marshall Blecher.

JAN HENRIK JANSEN ARKITEKTER

VILLA BONDÖ

VILLA BONDÖ

Gothenburg, Sweden
Photos: © Jan Töve

On the outskirts of Gothenburg, overlooking a beautiful lake surrounded by birch and pine, rests Villa Bondö, a family house with a seamless interior. Visible from the road, the facades use of larch and zinc roofing creates an anonymous appearance. The highlight of the design is the glass gable facing the lake, shielded from view as you arrive to the dwelling. Before entering the house, you can glimpse the lake through the glazed entrance but once inside you experience the breathtaking view as the building opens up to the panoramic view of the lake and the forest. The church-shaped volume of the dining hall and its structural glazing window become the centre of the interior experience. Throughout the process there was a close collaboration between the client and architect. All materials used in the house have been carefully discussed and designed to reach the vision of a minimalistic and aesthetic yet functional space for a family.

Am Stadtrand von Göteborg, mit Blick auf einen wunderschönen See, umgeben von Birken und Kiefern, liegt die Villa Bondö – ein Familienhaus mit einem fließenden und harmonischen Innenraum. Von der Straße aus sichtbar, verleihen ihr die Lärchenholzfassaden und das Zinkdach ein dezentes Erscheinungsbild. Das Highlight des Designs ist der verglaste Giebel mit Blick auf den See, der beim Ankommen verborgen bleibt. Schon vor dem Betreten des Hauses kann man den See durch den gläsernen Eingang erahnen, doch erst im Inneren entfaltet sich ein atemberaubendes Panorama von See und Wald. Der kirchenähnliche Essbereich mit seiner strukturellen Verglasung bildet das Zentrum des Innenraumerlebnisses. Während des gesamten Prozesses bestand eine enge Zusammenarbeit zwischen Kunde und Architekt. Alle verwendeten Materialien wurden sorgfältig ausgewählt und gestaltet, um die Vision eines minimalistischen, ästhetischen und funktionalen Raums für eine Familie zu verwirklichen.

À la périphérie de Göteborg, avec vue sur un magnifique lac entouré de bouleaux et de pins, se trouve la Villa Bondö, une maison familiale à l'intérieur fluide et harmonieux. Visible depuis la route, ses façades en mélèze et son toit en zinc lui confèrent une apparence discrète. Le point central du design est le pignon vitré donnant sur le lac, soigneusement dissimulé à l'arrivée. Avant d'entrer dans la maison, on aperçoit un premier aperçu du lac à travers l'entrée vitrée, mais une fois à l'intérieur, la vue s'ouvre spectaculairement sur le lac et la forêt environnante. Le volume en forme d'église de la salle à manger et sa grande baie vitrée deviennent le cœur de l'expérience intérieure. Tout au long du processus, une collaboration étroite entre le client et l'architecte a été essentielle. Tous les matériaux utilisés dans la maison ont été soigneusement sélectionnés et conçus pour atteindre la vision d'un espace familial minimaliste, esthétique et fonctionnel.

En las afueras de Gotemburgo, con vistas a un hermoso lago rodeado de abedules y pinos, se encuentra Villa Bondö, una casa familiar con un interior fluido y armonioso. Visible desde la carretera, sus fachadas de alerce y techo de zinc le otorgan una apariencia discreta. El punto culminante del diseño es el hastial acristalado que da al lago, protegido de la vista al llegar a la vivienda. Antes de entrar a la casa, se puede vislumbrar el lago a través de la entrada acristalada, pero una vez dentro, se experimenta una vista impresionante cuando el edificio se abre a un panorama del lago y el bosque. El volumen en forma de iglesia del comedor y su ventanal estructural se convierten en el centro de la experiencia interior. Durante todo el proceso, hubo una estrecha colaboración entre el cliente y el arquitecto. Todos los materiales utilizados en la casa han sido cuidadosamente seleccionados y diseñados para lograr la visión de un espacio minimalista, estético y funcional para una familia.

KAMINSKY ARKITEKTUR

Villa Bondö unveils its breathtaking lake views gradually, guiding visitors from a discreet larch façade to a soaring glass gable centerpiece.

TYFTET

TYFTET

Bollebygd, Sweden
Photos: © Jan Töve

In a forest on the outskirts of the city of Alingsås in Sweden, five climate-smart semi-detached houses are nestled harmoniously with the nature. The project incorporates a consistent focus on sustainability and a design with broken volumes strategically placed to complement the landscape.
The houses are certified as passive houses according to FEBY Gold standards. They also hold the Nordic Swan eco-label. Constructed with a timber frame, the houses feature integrated solar panels on the roof. The position around a shared courtyard offers a great space for a playground and cultivation areas.

In einem Wald am Rande der Stadt Alingsås in Schweden schmiegen sich fünf klimagerechte Doppelhaushälften harmonisch in die Natur. Das Projekt beinhaltet einen konsequenten Fokus auf Nachhaltigkeit und ein Design mit gebrochenen Volumen, die strategisch platziert sind, um die Landschaft zu ergänzen.
Die Häuser sind als Passivhäuser nach dem FEBY-Gold-Standard zertifiziert. Außerdem tragen sie das Umweltzeichen Nordic Swan. Die Häuser sind in Holzrahmenbauweise errichtet und verfügen über integrierte Sonnenkollektoren auf dem Dach. Die Lage um einen gemeinsamen Innenhof bietet viel Platz für einen Spielplatz und Anbauflächen.

Dans une forêt à la périphérie de la ville d'Alingsås en Suède, cinq maisons jumelées climatiquement intelligentes sont nichées harmonieusement dans la nature. Le projet intègre un accent constant sur la durabilité et un design avec des volumes brisés stratégiquement placés pour compléter le paysage.
Les maisons sont certifiées passives selon les normes FEBY Gold. Elles portent également l'éco-label nordique Swan. Construites avec une ossature en bois, les maisons sont dotées de panneaux solaires intégrés sur le toit. La disposition autour d'une cour commune offre un grand espace pour une aire de jeux et des zones de culture.

En un bosque a las afueras de la ciudad sueca de Alingsås, cinco casas adosadas climáticamente inteligentes se asientan en armonía con la naturaleza. El proyecto incorpora una atención constante a la sostenibilidad y un diseño con volúmenes quebrados estratégicamente situados para complementar el paisaje.
Las casas están certificadas como «Casas Pasivas» según las normas FEBY Gold. También tienen la etiqueta ecológica Nordic Swan. Construidas con un armazón de madera, las casas cuentan con paneles solares integrados en el tejado. La posición en torno a un patio compartido ofrece un gran espacio para un parque infantil y zonas de cultivo.

KAMINSKY ARKITEKTUR

WEEKEND HOUSE STRAUME

WEEKEND HOUSE STRAUME

Outside of Remøya, Norway
Photos: © Knut Hjeltnes

An old timber warehouse was washed away by a hurricane in 1992 leaving only the stone foundation intact. We were allowed to erect a new building, with the same volume, reusing the old foundations. It was decided to construct the complete 70 tons house on a nearby shipyard and lift it in place with an offshore crane. Seven steel frames establish the main construction, kept in place by the new concrete floor forming ground floor kitchen and living room. Four wooden volumes are mounted to these frames containing bathrooms, bedrooms and a media room. The attic is a large uninsulated storage space. Sheltered outdoor areas between the outer timber envelope and the proper insulated facade are used for outside work, dining, relaxation and all kinds of odd storage needed for fishing and other outdoor activities.

Ein altes Holzlager wurde 1992 von einem Hurrikan weggespült, wobei nur das steinerne Fundament intakt blieb. Wir durften ein neues Gebäude mit dem gleichen Volumen errichten, wobei die alten Fundamente wiederverwendet wurden. Wegen der schwierigen Baustelle wurde beschlossen, das komplette 70-Tonnen-Haus auf einer nahe gelegenen Werft zu errichten und mit einem Offshore-Kran an Ort und Stelle zu heben. Sieben Stahlrahmen bilden die Hauptkonstruktion, die durch den neuen Betonboden, der im Erdgeschoss Küche und Wohnzimmer bildet, an ihrem Platz gehalten wird. Auf diesen Rahmen sind vier Holzvolumina montiert, die Bäder, Schlafzimmer und einen Medienraum enthalten. Das Dachgeschoss ist ein großer, nicht isolierter Lagerraum. Geschützte Außenbereiche zwischen der äußeren Holzhülle und der entsprechend gedämmten Fassade werden für Arbeiten im Freien, Essen, Entspannung und alle Arten von unregelmäßigen Lagerräumen genutzt, die zum Angeln und für andere Aktivitäten im Freien benötigt werden.

Un ancien entrepôt de bois a été emporté par un ouragan en 1992, ne laissant que les fondations en pierre intactes. Nous avons été autorisés à construire un nouveau bâtiment, avec le même volume, en réutilisant les anciennes fondations. Il a été décidé de construire la maison complète de 70 tonnes sur un chantier naval voisin et de la soulever sur place avec une grue offshore. Sept charpentes en acier constituent la construction principale, maintenue en place par le nouveau sol en béton formant la cuisine et le salon du rez-dechaussée. Quatre volumes en bois sont montés sur ces charpentes, contenant des salles de bain, des chambres et une salle de presse. Le grenier est un grand espace de rangement non isolée. Les espaces extérieurs abrités entre l'enveloppe extérieure en bois et la façade isolée appropriée sont utilisés pour le travail extérieur, les repas, la détente et toutes sortes de rangements bizarres nécessaires à la pêche et à d'autres activités de plein air.

Un viejo almacén de madera fue arrastrado por un huracán en 1992 dejando sólo los cimientos de piedra intactos. Se nos permitió erigir un nuevo edificio, con el mismo volumen, reutilizando los viejos cimientos. Se decidió construir la casa completa de 70 toneladas en un astillero cercano y levantarla en su lugar con una grúa offshore. Siete marcos de acero establecen la construcción principal, mantenida en su lugar por el nuevo suelo de hormigón que forma la cocina y la sala de estar de la planta baja. Cuatro volúmenes de madera están montados en estos marcos que contienen baños, dormitorios y una sala de ocio. El ático es un gran espacio de almacenamiento sin aislamiento. Las áreas exteriores protegidas entre la envoltura exterior de madera y la fachada aislada adecuada se utilizan para el trabajo exterior, la cena, la relajación y todo tipo de almacenamiento extraño necesario para la pesca y otras actividades al aire libre.

KNUT HJELTNES

Balancing heritage and innovation, this reconstructed timber house integrates steel frames and prefabrication, seamlessly resting on its original stone foundation.

SALTVIGA HOUSE

SALTVIGA HOUSE

Saltviga, Norway
Photos: © Johan Dehlin

Built using over 12,000 recycled oak off-cuts, Saltviga House redefines sustainability and craftsmanship. The project transforms discarded wood into a striking cladding. Perched on a cliff along Norway's coast, the house follows the terrain's natural slope across multiple levels. Its oak façade will age to a silvery patina, while the Douglas-finished interior maintains a warm, subdued ambiance. Expansive windows capture panoramic views, fostering a seamless connection between architecture and landscape.

Mit über 12.000 recycelten Eichenholzstücken gebaut, ist Saltviga House ein Beispiel für nachhaltiges Handwerk. Das Projekt verwandelt Holzreste in eine einzigartige Fassade. Auf einer Klippe an Norwegens Küste gelegen, folgt das Haus der natürlichen Hanglage auf mehreren Ebenen. Die Eichenfassade wird mit der Zeit silbergrau, während das Douglas-Interieur eine warme Atmosphäre bewahrt. Panoramafenster rahmen die Landschaft ein und verbinden Architektur mit Natur.

Construite avec plus de 12 000 pièces de chêne recyclé, Saltviga House incarne la réutilisation et l'artisanat. Le projet transforme du bois destiné au rebut en un bardage unique. Perchée sur une falaise en Norvège, la maison suit la pente naturelle du terrain sur plusieurs niveaux. Sa façade en chêne vieillira en une patine argentée, tandis que l'intérieur en Douglas maintient une chaleur subtile. De grandes baies vitrées cadrent le paysage, intégrant harmonieusement l'architecture à son environnement.

Construida con más de 12.000 piezas de roble reciclado, Saltviga House es un ejercicio de reutilización y artesanía. El diseño nació del deseo de aprovechar recortes de madera destinados al descarte, transformándolos en un revestimiento único. Ubicada en un acantilado frente al mar en Noruega, la casa se adapta a la pendiente del terreno en diferentes niveles. Su fachada de roble envejecerá hasta volverse plateada, mientras que el interior, revestido en Douglas, mantiene una calidez sutil. Ventanales panorámicos enmarcan el paisaje, integrando la arquitectura con su entorno.

KOLMAN BOYE

Saltviga House repurposes 12,000 oak off-cuts into a dynamic façade that merges sustainability with craftsmanship along Norway's rugged coastal cliffs.

VEGA COTTAGE

VEGA COTTAGE

Vega Island, Norway
Photos: © Åke E:son Lindman

Located on Vega Island near the Arctic Circle, this cottage is inspired by traditional Norwegian Naust—seaside huts designed for resilience. Its aged, windowless wooden façade echoes the rugged landscape. Following the natural terrain, the house is accessed through a narrow rock passage. Inside, two compact yet spacious levels maximize the view. Large windows frame the ocean, mountains, and bedrock, while materials such as oiled pine and linoleum enhance its natural integration. The interior exudes a handcrafted character, emphasizing tactile quality and long-term patina.

Auf der Insel Vega, nahe dem Polarkreis, wurde diese Hütte von traditionellen norwegischen Naust inspiriert—schlichte, wetterfeste Küstenunterkünfte. Ihre gealterte, fensterlose Holzfassade spiegelt die raue Umgebung wider. Die natürliche Topografie bleibt erhalten, der Zugang erfolgt über eine schmale Felsspalte. Innen maximieren zwei kompakte, offene Ebenen den Raum. Große Fenster rahmen das Meer, die Berge und den Fels, während Materialien wie geölte Kiefer und Linoleum die natürliche Integration verstärken.

Situé sur l'île de Vega, près du cercle polaire, ce chalet s'inspire des Naust norvégiens traditionnels, des abris côtiers conçus pour résister aux éléments. Sa façade en bois vieilli et sans fenêtres reflète la robustesse du paysage. Suivant le relief naturel, l'accès se fait par une étroite faille rocheuse. L'intérieur, organisé sur deux niveaux compacts mais spacieux, maximise les vues. De grandes fenêtres cadrent l'océan, les montagnes et la roche, tandis que des matériaux comme le pin huilé et le linoléum renforcent l'harmonie avec la nature.

Ubicada en la isla de Vega, cerca del círculo polar, esta cabaña se inspira en las tradicionales Naust, refugios costeros noruegos. La estructura de madera envejecida y sin ventanas refleja el carácter robusto del paisaje. Diseñada para integrarse con su entorno, la casa sigue el relieve natural y se accede a través de una estrecha grieta rocosa. Su interior, organizado en dos niveles, ofrece espacios compactos pero generosos. Grandes ventanales enmarcan vistas del océano, las montañas y la roca circundante, mientras que materiales como pino aceitado y linóleo refuerzan la conexión con la naturaleza.

KOLMAN BOYE

Vega Cottage blends heritage and craftsmanship, reinterpreting traditional Norwegian Naust to create a resilient, landscape-integrated retreat.

LOST AND FOUND

VILLA HEDBERG

VILLA HEDBERG

Åhus, Sweden
Photos: © Johan Fowelin

In a serene setting where the beach meets the pines, Marge Architects were commissioned to design a summer house for a family of four. With neighbouring houses in close proximity to the north and south, and a public beach to the east, the brief was to create a truly private space for the client. As the family has its everyday life in the city, they needed a house that could be completely shut down during winter. By accommodating the wishes of the client on three different building briefs, a private house, a sauna and a guest house, a protected outdoor space was created, harbouring the family's need for privacy. From here, sightlines extend to the horizon and the sea, yet the characteristic roof remains the sole element visible from the beach.

In einer ruhigen Umgebung, wo der Strand auf die Kiefern trifft, wurden Marge Architects beauftragt, ein Sommerhaus für eine vierköpfige Familie zu entwerfen. Mit Nachbarhäusern in unmittelbarer Nähe im Norden und Süden und einem öffentlichen Strand im Osten bestand die Aufgabe darin, einen wirklich privaten Raum für den Bauherrn zu schaffen. Da die Familie ihren Alltag in der Stadt hat, brauchte sie ein Haus, das im Winter komplett stillgelegt werden kann. Durch die Berücksichtigung der Wünsche des Bauherrn auf drei verschiedenen Baustellen, einem Privathaus, einer Sauna und einem Gästehaus, wurde ein geschützter Außenraum geschaffen, der dem Bedürfnis der Familie nach Privatsphäre Rechnung trägt. Von hier aus reichen die Sichtachsen bis zum Horizont und zum Meer, wobei das charakteristische Dach das einzige vom Strand aus sichtbare Element bleibt.

Dans un cadre serein où la plage rencontre les pins, Marge Architects a été chargé de concevoir une maison d'été pour une famille de quatre personnes. Avec des maisons voisines à proximité immédiate au nord et au sud et une plage publique à l'est, la mission consistait à créer un espace véritablement privé pour le client. Comme la famille a sa vie quotidienne en ville, elle avait besoin d'une maison qui puisse être complètement fermée pendant l'hiver. En répondant aux souhaits du client sur trois projets de construction différents - une maison privée, un sauna et une maison d'hôtes - un espace extérieur protégé a été créé, respectant le besoin d'intimité de la famille. De là, les lignes de vue s'étendent jusqu'à l'horizon et la mer, mais le toit caractéristique reste le seul élément visible depuis la plage.

En un entorno sereno donde la playa se encuentra con los pinos, se encargó a Marge Arkitekter el diseño de una casa de verano para una familia de cuatro personas. Con las casas vecinas muy cerca del norte y del sur, y una playa pública al este, el encargo consistió en crear un espacio verdaderamente privado para el cliente. Como la familia tiene su vida cotidiana en la ciudad, necesitaban una casa que pudiera cerrarse completamente durante el invierno. En respuesta a los deseos del cliente, se construyeron una casa privada, una sauna y una casa de huéspedes en tres edificios diferentes, lo cual dio lugar a un espacio exterior protegido donde preservar la privacidad de la familia. Desde aquí, las líneas de visión se extienden hasta el horizonte y el mar, aunque el característico techo sigue siendo el único elemento visible desde la playa.

MARGE ARKITEKTER

A private retreat has been transformed into a coastal site where the architecture both protects and embraces the surrounding nature, with a spatially innovative design.

HOLIDAY HOME

HOLIDAY HOME

Archipelago of Stockholm, Sweden
Photos: © Åke E:son Lindman

The site where the four buildings are located consists of a beautiful meadow that slopes down to the sea. The level differences in the ground are reflected in the building's volume structures where floor levels and ceilings descend towards the sea. The façades are adorned with wooden panels painted with mud paint. Large glass sections of teak with sliding doors facing the sea make the boundary between the outside and the inside disappear. In the main building, the bedrooms are located on the highest level and a central living room, kitchen and dining area face panoramic views of the sea on the middle and lowest levels. A fireplace is located in the centre of the living area. Walls and ceilings and joinery are painted in white and the floors are covered with limestone and teak.

Das Gelände, auf dem sich die vier Gebäude befinden, besteht aus einer schönen Wiese, die zum Meer hin abfällt. Die Höhenunterschiede des Bodens spiegeln sich in den Volumenstrukturen des Gebäudes wider, wo Bodenebenen und Decken zum Meer hin abfallen. Die Fassaden sind mit Holztafeln geschmückt, die mit Schlammfarbe gestrichen sind. Große Glasflächen aus Teakholz mit Schiebetüren zum Meer hin lassen die Grenze zwischen außen und innen verschwinden. Im Hauptgebäude befinden sich die Schlafzimmer auf der höchsten Ebene und ein zentrales Wohnzimmer, Küche und Essbereich mit Panoramablick auf das Meer auf der mittleren und untersten Ebene. In der Mitte des Wohnbereichs befindet sich ein Kamin. Die Wände und Decken sowie die Tischlerarbeiten sind weiß gestrichen, und die Böden sind mit Kalkstein und Teakholz belegt.

Le site où se trouvent les quatre bâtiments est constitué d'une belle prairie qui descend en pente jusqu'à la mer. Les différences de niveau du sol se reflètent dans les structures volumétriques du bâtiment, où les niveaux des sols et des plafonds descendent vers la mer. Les façades sont ornées de panneaux en bois peints avec de la peinture à la boue. De grandes sections de verre en teck avec des portes coulissantes orientées vers la mer font disparaître la frontière entre l'extérieur et l'intérieur. Dans le bâtiment principal, les chambres sont situées au niveau le plus élevé et un salon central, une cuisine et une salle à manger font face à des vues panoramiques sur la mer aux niveaux intermédiaire et inférieur. Une cheminée est située au centre de la zone de séjour. Les murs, les plafonds et les menuiseries sont peints en blanc et les sols sont recouverts de calcaire et de teck.

El terreno donde se encuentran los cuatro edificios consiste en una hermosa pradera que desciende hasta el mar. Las diferencias de nivel se reflejan en las estructuras de volumen del edificio donde los niveles de suelo y techos descienden hacia el mar. Las fachadas están adornadas con paneles de madera pintados con pintura de barro. Grandes secciones de vidrio de teca con puertas corredizas que miran al mar hacen desaparecer el límite entre el exterior y el interior. En el edificio principal, los dormitorios están situados en el nivel más alto y una sala de estar central, la cocina y el comedor tienen vistas panorámicas al mar en los niveles medio y bajo. En el centro de la sala de estar hay una chimenea. Las paredes y los techos y la carpintería están pintados de blanco y los suelos están cubiertos de piedra caliza y teca.

MARGEN WIGOW ARKITEKTKONTOR

Descending towards the sea, these four pavilions blur boundaries with nature through sliding teak doors, mud-painted façades, and panoramic vistas.

PRIVATE SPA

PRIVATE SPA

Archipelago of Stockholm, Sweden
Photos: © Åke E:son Lidman

The spa is located in the archipelago of Stockholm. The aim has been to make the house feel part of nature. The simple rectangular volume is therefore placed low between two rock slabs. The roof consists of a floating concrete slab covered with grass and the large glass surfaces have surface-mounted wooden trellis whose climbing plants dress the house in vegetation. The entrance floor has pool room with an infinity pool, jacuzzi, relax, sauna and gym. Changing rooms, massage rooms and technical areas are located in the basement. Exterior materials, glass, wood and concrete reappear on the inside but have been supplemented with floors of Swedish limestone and slate, as well as oak carpentry. The private spa is done in collaboration with AC Sundberg Arkitekter and Bahri arkitekter.

Das Spa befindet sich im Stockholmer Archipel. Ziel war es, die Architektur harmonisch in die Natur zu integrieren. Deshalb wurde das rechteckige Volumen zwischen zwei Felsplatten platziert. Das Dach ist eine schwebende Betonplatte, die mit Gras bedeckt ist, und die großen Glasflächen sind mit Holzgittern versehen, die Kletterpflanzen tragen und das Gebäude mit Vegetation umhüllen. Im Erdgeschoss befinden sich ein Infinity-Pool, ein Whirlpool, eine Entspannungszone, eine Sauna und ein Fitnessraum. Umkleideräume, Massageräume und Technikbereiche sind im Untergeschoss untergebracht. Außenmaterialien wie Glas, Holz und Beton setzen sich auch im Innenraum fort und werden durch schwedische Kalkstein- und Schieferböden sowie Eichenholz ergänzt. Das private Spa wurde in Zusammenarbeit mit AC Sundberg Arkitekter und Bahri Arkitekter entworfen.

Le spa est situé dans l'archipel de Stockholm. L'objectif était d'intégrer la construction à la nature. Pour cela, le volume rectangulaire a été placé entre deux dalles rocheuses. Le toit est une dalle flottante en béton recouverte d'herbe, et les grandes surfaces vitrées sont équipées de treillis en bois supportant des plantes grimpantes, habillant ainsi la maison de végétation. Le rez-de-chaussée abrite la piscine à débordement, le jacuzzi, l'espace de détente, le sauna et la salle de sport. Les vestiaires, les salles de massage et les espaces techniques se trouvent au sous-sol. Les matériaux extérieurs, tels que le verre, le bois et le béton, sont également utilisés à l'intérieur, complétés par des sols en calcaire suédois et en ardoise, ainsi que des menuiseries en chêne. Le «spa privé» a été conçu en collaboration avec AC Sundberg Arkitekter et Bahri Arkitekter.

El spa se encuentra en el archipiélago de Estocolmo. El objetivo ha sido integrar la construcción con la naturaleza. Por ello, el volumen rectangular se ha ubicado entre dos losas de roca. El techo es una losa de hormigón flotante cubierta de hierba, y las grandes superficies acristaladas cuentan con celosías de madera que soportan plantas trepadoras, vistiendo la casa con vegetación. La planta de acceso alberga la piscina infinita, jacuzzi, zona de relax, sauna y gimnasio. Los vestuarios, salas de masajes y áreas técnicas se encuentran en el sótano. Los materiales exteriores, como vidrio, madera y hormigón, también se emplean en el interior, complementados con suelos de piedra caliza sueca y pizarra, además de carpintería de roble. El spa privado ha sido diseñado en colaboración con AC Sundberg Arkitekter y Bahri Arkitekter.

MARGEN WIGOW ARKITEKTKONTOR

SEASIDE CABINS

SEASIDE CABINS

Archipelago of Stockholm, Sweden
Photos: © Åke E:son Lindman

The island is located at the far end of Stockholm's outer archipelago. The new buildings are built in a valley facing a sheltered bay. The wish has been to create a modern variant of the older shanty towns, which still today remain on individual islands in Stockholm.
The direction of the houses and the slope of the roof follow the shape of the mountains and are covered with sedum roofs. The façades are lined with wooden panels painted with mud paint. The main building consists of a single large room where each function is divided by the different floor levels made of solid pine boards. The walls, ceilings and furnishings are made of pine plywood. On the island there is no electricity so all houses have a fireplace for heating, refrigerator and stove powered by gas, lamps of kerosene and water pumped up by hand outdoors.

Die Insel liegt am äußersten Ende des Stockholmer Außenschärengartens. Die neuen Gebäude sind in einem Tal mit Blick auf eine geschützte Bucht gebaut. Der Wunsch war es, eine moderne Variante der älteren Barackensiedlungen zu schaffen, die heute noch auf einzelnen Inseln in Stockholm stehen.
Die Ausrichtung der Häuser und die Neigung des Daches folgen der Form der Berge. Sie sind mit Sedumdächern gedeckt. Die Fassaden sind mit Holztafeln verkleidet, die mit Lehmfarbe gestrichen sind. Das Hauptgebäude besteht aus einem einzigen großen Raum, in dem jede Funktion durch die verschiedenen Geschossebenen aus massiven Kiefernbrettern unterteilt ist. Die Wände, Decken und Einrichtungsgegenstände sind aus Kiefernsperrholz gefertigt. Auf der Insel gibt es keine Elektrizität, daher verfügen alle Häuser über einen Kamin zum Heizen, Kühlschrank und Herd, die mit Gas betrieben werden, Lampen mit Kerosin und Wasser, die von Hand ins Freie gepumpt werden.

L'île est située à l'extrémité de l'archipel extérieur de Stockholm. Les nouveaux bâtiments sont construits dans une vallée qui fait face à une baie abritée. Le souhait a été de créer une variante moderne des anciens bidonvilles, qui se trouvent encore aujourd'hui sur des îles individuelles de Stockholm.
L'orientation des maisons et la pente du toit suivent la forme des montagnes et sont recouvertes de toits de sedum. Les façades sont revêtues de panneaux de bois peints avec de la peinture à la boue. Le bâtiment principal est constitué d'une seule grande pièce où chaque fonction est divisée par les différents niveaux de plancher en planches de pin massif. Les murs, les plafonds et le mobilier sont en contreplaqué de pin. Sur l'île, il n'y a pas d'électricité, donc toutes les maisons ont une cheminée pour le chauffage, un réfrigérateur et une cuisinière au gaz, des lampes au kérosène et de l'eau pompée à la main à l'extérieur.

La isla está situada en el extremo más alejado del archipiélago exterior de Estocolmo. Los nuevos edificios están construidos en un valle que da a una bahía protegida. Se ha querido crear una variante moderna de los antiguos barrios de chabolas, que aún hoy permanecen en ciertas islas de Estocolmo.
La dirección de las casas y la inclinación del tejado siguen la forma de las montañas y están cubiertas con tejados de sedum. Las fachadas están revestidas con paneles de madera pintados con pintura de barro. El edificio principal consiste en una única habitación grande donde cada función está dividida por los diferentes niveles del suelo hechos de tableros de pino macizo. Las paredes, los techos y los muebles están hechos de contrachapado de pino. En la isla no hay electricidad, por lo que todas las casas tienen una chimenea para la calefacción, un refrigerador y una estufa que funcionan con gas, lámparas de queroseno y agua bombeada a mano en el exterior.

MARGEN WIGOW ARKITEKTKONTOR

Inspired by historic shanty towns, these off-grid cabins merge with the landscape, their sedum roofs and timber façades echoing the island's natural forms.

VILLA RYYSYRANTA II

VILLA RYYSYRANTA II

Finland
Photos: © Arno de la Chapelle

Villa Ryysyranta II is an evolution of an earlier design with the same principles of maintaining a delicate balance between the fragile beach landscape and tradition-based contemporary architecture. The sparse placement, scale and shape of the building masses and material choices with transparent design throughout root the building firmly with its surroundings. The enjoyment of the outdoors is maximized throughout the seasons.

Die Villa Ryysyranta II ist eine Weiterentwicklung eines früheren Entwurfs mit den gleichen Prinzipien der Aufrechterhaltung eines empfindlichen Gleichgewichts zwischen der fragilen Strandlandschaft und traditionsbasierter zeitgenössischer Architektur. Die spärliche Platzierung, der Maßstab und die Form der Gebäudemassen und die Materialwahl mit durchgehend transparentem Design verwurzeln das Gebäude fest in seiner Umgebung. Die Freude an der Natur wird zu jeder Jahreszeit maximiert.

La Villa Ryysyranta II est l'évolution d'une conception antérieure, avec les mêmes principes de maintien d'un équilibre délicat entre le paysage fragile de plage et l'architecture contemporaine basée sur la tradition. L'emplacement, l'échelle, la forme des masses du bâtiment et le choix des matériaux, ainsi que la transparence de la conception tout au long de la construction, ancrent fermement le bâtiment dans son environnement. Le plaisir de la vie en plein air est maximisé au fil des saisons.

Villa Ryysyranta II es una evolución de un diseño anterior con los mismos principios de mantener un delicado equilibrio entre el frágil paisaje de la playa y la arquitectura contemporánea basada en la tradición. El escaso volumen, escala y forma de los edificios y las elecciones de materiales con diseño transparente en todo el conjunto lo arraigan firmemente a su entorno. El disfrute del aire libre se maximiza a lo largo de las estaciones del año.

PAVE ARCHITECTS

Balancing tradition and innovation, it seamlessly integrates with its coastal setting, maximizing outdoor living across all seasons.

VILLA VOID

Viken, Norway
Photos: © Olav Resell

Sitting on sloping terrain, the house is surrounded by tall pine trees. It has an elongated main volume inspired by other houses in the area, from which parts has been subtracted to meet functional needs. The materiality underlines this concept, with the basic shape given a precise surface enhancing its sculptural qualities, and the recessed parts held in a warmer material with more visual depth.
The interior is characterized by a longitudinal main space containing living room, kitchen and dining room. These spaces are visually connected, but sit on different levels, with each one corresponding to the outside terrain. A narrow void spans a large portion of the buildings length, providing visual contact between levels, and bringing daylight down onto the back wall of the main space.

Das Haus steht auf abschüssigem Gelände und ist von hohen Pinienbäumen umgeben. Es hat ein langgestrecktes Hauptvolumen, das von anderen Häusern in der Gegend inspiriert ist und von dem Teile abgetrennt wurden, um funktionellen Bedürfnissen gerecht zu werden. Die Materialität unterstreicht dieses Konzept, wobei die Grundform eine präzise Oberfläche erhält, die ihre skulpturalen Qualitäten verstärkt, und die zurückgesetzten Teile in einem wärmeren Material mit mehr visueller Tiefe gehalten sind.
Das Innere ist durch einen länglichen Hauptraum gekennzeichnet, der Wohnzimmer, Küche und Esszimmer enthält. Diese Räume sind visuell miteinander verbunden, befinden sich aber auf verschiedenen Ebenen, die jeweils dem Außengelände entsprechen. Ein schmaler Hohlraum überspannt einen großen Teil der Gebäudelänge, bietet Sichtkontakt zwischen den Ebenen und bringt Tageslicht auf die Rückwand des Hauptraumes.

Située sur un terrain en pente, la maison est entourée de grands pins. Elle possède un volume principal allongé inspiré des autres maisons de la région, dont certaines parties ont été soustraites pour répondre à des besoins fonctionnels. La matérialité souligne ce concept, la forme de base étant dotée d'une surface précise qui renforce ses qualités sculpturales et les parties en retrait étant maintenues dans un matériau plus chaud avec plus de profondeur visuelle.
L'intérieur est caractérisé par un espace principal longitudinal contenant le salon, la cuisine et la salle à manger. Ces espaces sont visuellement reliés, mais se situent à des niveaux différents, chacun correspondant au terrain extérieur. Un vide étroit s'étend sur une grande partie de la longueur des bâtiments, assurant un contact visuel entre les niveaux et faisant descendre la lumière du jour sur le mur arrière de l'espace principal.

Asentada en un terreno inclinado, la casa está rodeada de altos pinos. Tiene un volumen principal alargado inspirado en otras casas de la zona, del que se han sustraído partes para satisfacer las necesidades funcionales. La materialidad subraya este concepto, con la forma básica a la que se da una superficie precisa que realza sus cualidades escultóricas, y las partes empotradas sostenidas en un material más cálido con más profundidad visual.
El interior se caracteriza por un espacio principal longitudinal que contiene la sala de estar, la cocina y el comedor. Estos espacios están visualmente conectados, pero se sitúan en diferentes niveles, relacionado cada uno de ellos al terreno exterior. Un estrecho vacío abarca una gran parte de la longitud de los edificios, proporcionando contacto visual entre los niveles y llevando la luz natural a la pared trasera del espacio principal.

RESELL+NICCA

CABIN RYFYLKE

CABIN RYFYLKE

Ryfylke, Norway
Photos: © Olav Resell

The cabin is situated in a gently sloping terrain on a small and lush island in the western part of Norway. Its enclosing form creates a protected and sunny outdoor space with views over the fjord to the south. Common spaces caters onto this side, while secondary rooms are located on the opposite side facing the forest. A dark, diamond shaped Norwegian slate stone is used on the façade, with format sizes pushed towards the maximum of what is possible to extract. Ash is chosen as the main interior material, and used as panelling on ceiling and walls, plywood on walls and solid furnishings, and as solid wood flooring on the upper level. A key element in the cabin is the concrete structure at the center. It is cast with horizontal panelling formwork, and acts as an important heat storage element.

Die Hütte liegt in einem sanft abfallenden Gelände auf einer kleinen, üppig bewachsenen Insel im westlichen Teil Norwegens. Ihre umschließende Form schafft einen geschützten und sonnigen Außenraum mit Blick über den Fjord nach Süden. Auf dieser Seite befinden sich die Gemeinschaftsräume, während die Nebenräume auf der gegenüberliegenden, dem Wald zugewandten Seite liegen. An der Fassade wird ein dunkler, rautenförmiger norwegischer Schieferstein verwendet, wobei die Formatgrößen auf das Maximum dessen, was gewonnen werden kann, ausgerichtet sind. Als Hauptmaterial für den Innenraum wurde Esche gewählt, die als Vertäfelung an Decke und Wänden, als Sperrholz an Wänden und massiven Einrichtungsgegenständen sowie als Massivholzboden im oberen Stockwerk verwendet wird. Ein Schlüsselelement in der Hütte ist die Betonstruktur in der Mitte.

Sie ist mit horizontalen Schalungstafeln gegossen und dient als wichtiges Wärmespeicherelement. La cabane est située dans un terrain en pente douce sur une petite île luxuriante dans la partie occidentale de la Norvège. Sa forme enveloppante crée un espace extérieur protégé et ensoleillé avec des vues sur le fjord au sud. Les espaces communs se trouvent de ce côté, tandis que les pièces secondaires sont situées sur le côté opposé, face à la forêt. Une pierre d'ardcise norvégienne sombre en forme de diamant est utilisée sur la façade, les formats étant poussés au maximum de ce qu'il est possible d'extraire. Le frêne est choisi comme principal matériau intérieur et utilisé comme lambris au plafond et sur les murs, comme contreplaqué sur les murs et le mobilier solide et comme plancher en bois massif au niveau supérieur. La structure en béton au centre est un élément clé de la cabine. Elle est coulée avec un coffrage de lambris horizontal et agit comme un élément important de stockage de la chaleur.

La cabaña está situada en un terreno de suave pendiente en una pequeña y exuberante isla en la parte occidental de Noruega. Su forma envolvente crea un espacio exterior protegido y soleado con vistas al fiordo del sur. Los espacios comunes se encuentran en este lado, mientras que las habitaciones secundarias se encuentran en el lado opuesto, frente al bosque. En la fachada se utiliza una piedra oscura de pizarra noruega en forma de diamante. Se elige el fresno como principal material en el interior, y se utiliza como revestimiento en el techo y las paredes. La madera contrachapada se ha utilizado también en las paredes y el mobiliario. El suelo del nivel superior es madera maciza. Un elemento esencial de la cabaña es la estructura central de hormigón, fundida con encofrado de paneles horizontales, y que actúa como importante elemento de almacenamiento de calor.

RESELL+NICCA

Nestled on a lush Norwegian island, this slate-clad retreat frames fjord views while a central concrete core anchors warmth and stability.

MANSHAUSEN

MANSHAUSEN

Steigen Archipelago, Norway
Photos: © Kjell Ove Storvik, Steve King, Siggen Stinessen

Manshausen Island is situated in the Steigen Archipelago off the coast of northern Norway and is home to the world´s largest population of sea eagles. The Island´s position between majestic mountains and the Barents Sea is in itself the inspiration for the design.
The resort is organized with guestrooms as individual cabins placed at the top of the rocky formations of the Island, where the positioning in the landscape ensures an immersive, yet private, view to the majestic nature and the elements outside. The shelter design endeavours to make a minimum environmental impact with minimum footprint and the use of cross laminated timber construction. The old farmhouse was renovated and converted to restaurant and library. A sauna was made in the natural pond using left over materials.

Die Insel Manshausen liegt im Steigen-Archipel vor der Küste Nordnorwegens und beheimatet die größte Seeadlerpopulation der Welt. Die Lage der Insel zwischen majestätischen Bergen und der Barentssee ist an sich schon die Inspiration für das Design.
Das Resort ist mit Gästezimmern als Einzelkabinen organisiert, die auf der Spitze der Felsformationen der Insel platziert sind, wo die Positionierung in der Landschaft einen eindringlichen, aber dennoch privaten Blick auf die majestätische Natur und die Elemente draußen gewährleistet. Bei der Gestaltung der Unterkünfte wird versucht, die Umwelt so wenig wie möglich zu belasten, mit minimalem Platzbedarf und dem Einsatz von Brettsperrholzkonstruktionen. Das alte Bauernhaus wurde renoviert und zu einem Restaurant und einer Bibliothek umgebaut. Im Naturteich wurde eine Sauna aus Materialresten errichtet.

L'île de Manshausen est située dans l'archipel de Steigen, au large des côtes du nord de la Norvège et abrite la plus grande population d'aigles de mer du monde. La position de l'île, entre des montagnes majestueuses et la mer de Barents, est une véritable source d'inspiration pour le projet.
La station est organisée en chambres d'hôtes sous forme de cabines individuelles placées au sommet des formations rocheuses de l'île, où le positionnement dans le paysage assure une vue immersive, mais privée, sur la nature majestueuse et les éléments extérieurs. La conception de l'abri s'efforce d'avoir un impact minimal sur l'environnement avec une empreinte minimale et l'utilisation de constructions en bois lamellé croisé. L'ancienne ferme a été rénovée et transformée en restaurant et en bibliothèque. Un sauna a été réalisé dans l'étang naturel en utilisant des restes de matériaux.

La isla de Manshausen está situada en el archipiélago Steigen, frente a la costa del norte de Noruega, y alberga la mayor población mundial de gaviotas. La posición de la isla entre las majestuosas montañas y el mar de Barents fue en sí misma la inspiración para el diseño.
El complejo está organizado con habitaciones de huéspedes como cabañas individuales situadas en la cima de las formaciones rocosas de la isla, donde la ubicación en el paisaje asegura una vista amplia, aunque privada, de la majestuosa naturaleza y el exterior. En el diseño de las cabañas se procura que el impacto ambiental sea mínimo utilizando una construcción de madera laminada en cruz. La antigua granja fue renovada y convertida en restaurante y biblioteca. Se hizo una sauna en el estanque natural usando los materiales sobrantes.

STINESSEN ARKITEKTUR

Perched on rocky cliffs, Manshausen's cabins immerse guests in Norway's wild beauty, blending sustainability with an uninterrupted dialogue between land and sea.

EFJORD

EFJORD

Lofoten Fiord, Norway
Photos: © Snorre Stinessen, Steve King

Efjord is a branch off the Lofoten fiord in northern Norway. The client wanted a retreat that focused on the panoramic views of the site, but which also transported them to a feeling of isolation and total privacy, away from hectic working days in the city. The conceptual layout opens and closes the building in different directions, where the eastern part of the cabin closes towards some neighbouring buildings and opens towards a ridge and the terrain on the other side. The opposite directions are sought at the front end of the cabin, opening up to the magnificent views towards the dramatic mountains and the fiord to the west. The two volumes are slightly offset to provide for sheltered outdoor areas and views towards the fiord also from the rear volume.

Der Efjord ist ein Seitenarm des Lofotenfjords in Nordnorwegen. Der Bauherr wünschte sich einen Rückzugsort, der sich auf die Panoramablicke des Ortes konzentriert, aber auch ein Gefühl der Isolation und der totalen Privatsphäre vermittelt, fernab von hektischen Arbeitstagen in der Stadt. Das konzeptionelle Layout öffnet und schließt das Gebäude in verschiedene Richtungen, wobei sich der östliche Teil der Hütte zu einigen Nachbargebäuden hin schließt und sich zu einem Bergrücken und dem Gelände auf der anderen Seite hin öffnet. Am vorderen Ende der Hütte werden die entgegengesetzten Richtungen gesucht, die sich zu den herrlichen Aussichten auf die dramatischen Berge und den Fjord im Westen hin öffnen. Die beiden Volumina sind leicht versetzt, um geschützte Außenbereiche und Ausblicke auf den Fjord auch vom hinteren Volumen aus zu ermöglichen.

L'Efjord est une branche du fjord d'Lofoten, dans le nord de la Norvège. Le client souhaitait une retraite axée sur les vues panoramiques du site, mais qui procure également un sentiment d'isolement et d'intimité totale, loin des journées de travail trépidantes de la ville. Le plan conceptuel ouvre et ferme le bâtiment dans différentes directions. La partie orientale de la cabane se ferme vers certains bâtiments voisins et s'ouvre vers une crête et le terrain de l'autre côté. Les directions opposées sont recherchées à l'extrémité avant de la cabane, s'ouvrant sur les vues magnifiques vers les montagnes spectaculaires et le fjord à l'ouest. Les deux volumes sont légèrement décalés pour permettre d'abriter les espaces extérieurs et d'offrir des vues vers le fjord également depuis le volume arrière.

Efjord es una rama del fiordo de Lofoten en el norte de Noruega. El cliente deseaba un retiro que se centrara en las vistas panorámicas del lugar, pero que también los transportara a una sensación de aislamiento y total privacidad, lejos de los agitados días de trabajo en la ciudad. La disposición conceptual abre y cierra el edificio en diferentes direcciones, donde la parte oriental de la cabaña se cierra hacia algunos edificios vecinos y se abre hacia una cresta y el terreno vecino. En el extremo delantero de la cabaña se buscan las direcciones opuestas, abriéndose a las magníficas vistas hacia las dramáticas montañas y el fiordo al oeste. Los dos volúmenes están ligeramente compensados para proporcionar zonas exteriores protegidas y vistas hacia el fiordo incluso desde el volumen trasero.

STINESSEN ARKITEKTUR

MALANGEN

MALANGEN

Mortenhals, Tromsø, Norway
Photos: © Stefano Lodola, Terje Arntsen, Steve King

The clients, a family with small children, wanted room for the larger family and friends. The conceptual layout was conceived as several individual volumes connected via in-between spaces and a central winter garden placed on a natural shelf in the land. The organisation provides both privacy and room for several activities at the same time. The central winter garden, with fireplace and outdoor kitchen, function as the entrance to the building. From here the retreat opens up to the natural clearing in the forest, entering into either the main building or the annex. Each group of rooms are conceived as separate volumes to achieve an additional layer of privacy, but also to emphasize the transition between spaces and activities while telling a story of everyday journeys.

Die Kunden, eine Familie mit kleinen Kindern, wollten Platz für die größere Familie und Freunde. Das konzeptionelle Layout wurde als mehrere Einzelvolumina konzipiert, die durch Zwischenräume und einen zentralen Wintergarten auf einer natürlichen Anhöhe im Land verbunden sind. Die Organisation bietet sowohl Privatsphäre als auch Raum für mehrere Aktivitäten zur gleichen Zeit. Der zentrale Wintergarten mit Kamin und Außenküche fungiert als Eingang zum Gebäude. Von hier aus öffnet sich der Rückzugsraum zur natürlichen Lichtung im Wald und führt entweder in das Hauptgebäude oder in den Anbau. Jede Raumgruppe ist als separates Volumen konzipiert, um eine zusätzliche Ebene der Privatsphäre zu erreichen, aber auch, um den Übergang zwischen Räumen und Aktivitäten zu betonen und gleichzeitig eine Geschichte der alltäglichen Wege zu erzählen.

Les clients - une famille avec de jeunes enfants - voulaient de la place pour la grande famille et les amis. L'agencement conceptuel a été conçu en plusieurs volumes individuels reliés par des espaces intermédiaires et un jardin d'hiver central, placé sur une étagère naturelle dans le terrain. L'organisation offre à la fois de l'intimité et de la place pour plusieurs activités en même temps. Le jardin d'hiver central, avec sa cheminée et sa cuisine extérieure, sert d'entrée au bâtiment. De là, la retraite s'ouvre sur la clairière naturelle de la forêt, en entrant soit dans le bâtiment principal, soit dans l'annexe. Chaque groupe de pièces est conçu comme un volume séparé pour obtenir une couche supplémentaire d'intimité, mais aussi pour souligner la transition entre les espaces et les activités tout en racontant une histoire de voyages quotidiens.

Los clientes, una familia con niños pequeños, necesitaban más espacio. La disposición conceptual fue concebida como varios volúmenes individuales conectados a través de espacios intermedios y un jardín de invierno central colocado en un estante natural en el terreno. La organización proporciona tanto privacidad como espacio para varias actividades al mismo tiempo. El jardín de invierno, con chimenea y cocina exterior, funciona como entrada al edificio. Desde aquí el refugio se abre al claro natural del bosque, entrando en el edificio principal o en el anexo. Cada grupo de habitaciones se concibe como volúmenes separados para lograr privacidad adicional, pero también para enfatizar la transición entre los espacios y actividades.

STINESSEN ARKITEKTUR

ROCK THE SHACK

An immersive retreat where architecture and nature merge in fluid spaces that balance privacy, community and a deep connection to place.

VILLA TORÖ

VILLA TORÖ

Archipelago of Stockholm, Sweden
Photos: © Åke E:son Lindman, Trigueiros Architecture

The cliff landscape, minerally ground, organic pine trees and heavy winds gives form to Villa Torö. Its positioning at a ridge of the cliff landscape in Stockholm archipelago offers a generous view above the treetops. Ruff cedar wooden boards contrast the enclosed refined concrete shape. Magical pine trees follow the buildings' confident posture. Its graphic play between shapes and materials creates a dynamic yet monolithic shape and breaks up the large volume into a smaller scale. The materials on the outside continues to the interior. Mineral walls and wooden surfaces interplay throughout the house. Carefully crafted furniture picks up the colours of surroundings becoming one with the framed views. Each room with its own quality in relation to the outside; closeness to the rock, spaces among the treetops, hidden niches and a sunny atrium creating a haven from the harsh winds.

Die felsige Landschaft, der mineralische Boden, die organisch gewachsenen Kiefern und die starken Winde prägen Villa Torö. Ihre Lage auf dem Kamm einer Klippe im Stockholmer Archipel bietet einen großzügigen Blick über die Baumwipfel. Die rauen Zedernholzbretter kontrastieren mit der geschlossenen Form des veredelten Betons. Magische Kiefern begleiten die selbstbewusste Haltung des Gebäudes. Das grafische Spiel zwischen Formen und Materialien schafft eine dynamische, aber monolithische Struktur, die das große Volumen in eine kleinere, harmonische Maßstäblichkeit auflöst. Die Außenmaterialien setzen sich im Innenraum fort: Mineralische Wände und Holzflächen ziehen sich durch das gesamte Haus. Sorgfältig gestaltete Möbel fangen die Farben der Umgebung ein und verschmelzen mit den gerahmten Ausblicken. Jeder Raum hat seine eigene Qualität in Bezug auf das Äußere: die Nähe zum Fels, die offenen Räume zwischen den Baumwipfeln, versteckte Nischen und ein sonniger Innenhof, der Schutz vor den starken Winden bietet.

Le paysage rocheux, le sol minéral, les pins organiques et les vents forts façonnent la Villa Torö. Située au sommet d'une falaise dans l'archipel de Stockholm, elle offre une vue dégagée au-dessus des cimes des arbres. Les planches rugueuses en cèdre contrastent avec la forme fermée du béton raffiné. Des pins majestueux accompagnent la silhouette affirmée des bâtiments. Le jeu graphique entre formes et matériaux crée une structure dynamique mais monolithique, décomposant le volume imposant en une échelle plus intime. Les matériaux extérieurs se prolongent à l'intérieur : murs minéraux et surfaces en bois se combinent dans toute la maison. Le mobilier soigneusement conçu capte les teintes de l'environnement et se fond dans les vues encadrées. Chaque pièce possède une qualité unique en relation avec l'extérieur : proximité de la roche, espaces entre les cimes des arbres, niches cachées et un atrium ensoleillé offrant un refuge contre les vents violents.

El paisaje rocoso, el suelo mineral, los pinos orgánicos y los fuertes vientos dan forma a Villa Torö. Su ubicación en la cresta de un acantilado en el archipiélago de Estocolmo ofrece una vista generosa por encima de las copas de los árboles. Las tablas rugosas de madera de cedro contrastan con la forma cerrada de hormigón refinado. Mágicos pinos acompañan la postura segura de los edificios. Su juego gráfico entre formas y materiales crea una estructura dinámica pero monolítica, descomponiendo el gran volumen en una escala más pequeña. Los materiales exteriores continúan en el interior: muros minerales y superficies de madera se combinan en toda la casa. Los muebles cuidadosamente diseñados capturan los colores del entorno y se funden con las vistas enmarcadas. Cada habitación tiene su propia cualidad en relación con el exterior: proximidad a la roca, espacios entre las copas de los árboles, nichos ocultos y un atrio soleado que ofrece refugio contra los fuertes vientos.

TRIGUEIROS ARCHITECTURE

Villa Torö fuses Scandinavian heritage with bold contrasts of materials in a sculptural dialogue between cliff, wind and pine trees.

CONE HOUSE

CONE HOUSE

Archipelago of Stockholm, Sweden
Photos: © Åke E:son Lindman, Trigueiros Architecture

Sloping like the site it sits on the Cone House playfully adjusts to its surrounding in the Stockholm archipelago. The building seems to be stretching down towards the water just meters away. The challenges of the modern shape draped in a traditional cedar chip facade is met by great craftsmanship with its carefully executed details. The technic rooted in the traditional wood chip church facades is in this project given a new take. Both expressive yet minimalistic the shape conceals a dynamic interior where ceiling height varies from 2,5 to 7,5 meters. Entering the house, a landscape of spaces on different levels is revealed opening up towards the water. Like a backbone the straight oak stair spans the full length of the house connecting all spaces from the south porch to the north porch. A minimalistic light interior clad with parts in oak wood and Swedish marble creates an honest interior.

In Anlehnung an das Gelände, auf dem sie steht, fügt sich Casa Cono spielerisch in ihre Umgebung im Stockholmer Archipel ein. Das Gebäude scheint sich zum Wasser hin zu strecken – nur wenige Meter entfernt. Die Herausforderungen der modernen Form, verkleidet mit einer traditionellen Zedernschindelfassade, wurden mit großer Meisterschaft und akribischer Detailgenauigkeit gelöst. Die Technik, die in traditionellen, mit Holzschindeln verkleideten Kirchenfassaden verwurzelt ist, wird hier neu interpretiert. Ausdrucksstark, aber minimalistisch verbirgt die Form ein dynamisches Inneres, in dem die Deckenhöhe zwischen 2,5 und 7,5 Metern variiert. Beim Betreten des Hauses entfaltet sich eine Landschaft aus Räumen auf verschiedenen Ebenen, die sich zum Wasser hin öffnen. Wie eine Wirbelsäule durchzieht eine gerade Eichenholztreppe das gesamte Haus und verbindet alle Bereiche vom Süd- bis zum Nordbalkon. Ein heller, minimalistischer Innenraum, teilweise mit Eichenholz und schwedischem Marmor verkleidet, schafft eine ehrliche und einladende Atmosphäre.

S'inclinant comme le terrain sur lequel elle repose, la Maison Cono s'adapte de manière ludique à son environnement dans l'archipel de Stockholm. Le bâtiment semble s'étirer vers l'eau, à seulement quelques mètres de distance. Les défis liés à sa forme moderne, revêtue d'une façade traditionnelle en bardeaux de cèdre, sont relevés avec une grande maîtrise et une exécution méticuleuse des détails. La technique, ancrée dans les façades traditionnelles des églises revêtues de bardeaux de bois, est ici réinterprétée. Expressive mais minimaliste, sa forme dissimule un intérieur dynamique, où la hauteur sous plafond varie entre 2,5 et 7,5 mètres. En entrant dans la maison, on découvre un paysage d'espaces disposés à différents niveaux, s'ouvrant vers l'eau. Comme une colonne vertébrale, un escalier droit en chêne traverse toute la longueur de la maison, reliant tous les espaces, du porche sud au porche nord. Un intérieur lumineux et minimaliste, partiellement revêtu de chêne et de marbre suédois, crée une atmosphère à la fois authentique et accueillante.

Inclinándose como el terreno sobre el que se asienta, la Casa Cono se adapta de manera lúdica a su entorno en el archipiélago de Estocolmo. El edificio parece estirarse hacia el agua, a solo unos metros de distancia. Los desafíos de su forma moderna, revestida con una fachada tradicional de tejas de cedro, son superados con gran maestría y una ejecución meticulosa de los detalles. La técnica, arraigada en las fachadas tradicionales de iglesias revestidas con tejas de madera, recibe aquí una reinterpretación. Expresiva pero minimalista, su forma oculta un interior dinámico, donde la altura del techo varía entre 2,5 y 7,5 metros. Al entrar en la casa, se revela un paisaje de espacios en diferentes niveles que se abren hacia el agua. Como una columna vertebral, una escalera recta de roble recorre toda la longitud de la casa, conectando todos los espacios desde el porche sur hasta el porche norte. Un interior luminoso y minimalista, revestido en partes de madera de roble y mármol sueco, crea una atmósfera honesta y acogedora.

TRIGUEIROS ARCHITECTURE

Cone House cascades towards the water, its cedar-clad form blending tradition with innovation, while a central oak stair unites its dynamic spaces.

VILLA LILLVIKEN

VILLA LILLVIKEN

Ångermanland, Sweden
Photos: © Trigueiros Architecture

Like an erratic block tucked in a crevice of the cliff, the building blends in with its surrounding. The endless force of nature has shaped the rocks creating a sheltered space from the southeast ocean storms. With time it will also drain the colours of the wood giving it the same silvery tones as the surrounding rocks. The changing seasons of the scenery outside is present in every room through the large glass surfaces as well as smaller carefully framed views bringing the nature into the house. The closeness to the raging waves from the inside gives the feeling of being at sea. Inside colours and materials are carefully picked to create a calm entity. Bricks from the north of Sweden, linen textiles and oak wood. Together with the carefully crafted furniture the interior has a strong Scandinavian root with an international touch.

Wie ein Findling, der in einer Felsspalte steckt, fügt sich das Gebäude in seine Umgebung ein. Die unaufhörliche Kraft der Natur hat die Felsen geformt und einen geschützten Zufluchtsort vor den Stürmen des südöstlichen Ozeans geschaffen. Mit der Zeit wird auch das Holz seine Farbe verlieren und die gleichen silbernen Töne wie die umgebenden Felsen annehmen. Die wechselnden Jahreszeiten der Landschaft sind in jedem Raum präsent – durch große Glasflächen und sorgfältig gerahmte Ausblicke, die die Natur nach innen holen. Die Nähe zu den tosenden Wellen vermittelt von innen das Gefühl, sich direkt auf dem Meer zu befinden. Farben und Materialien im Inneren wurden sorgfältig ausgewählt, um eine ruhige Einheit zu schaffen: Ziegel aus Nordschweden, Leinentextilien und Eichenholz. Zusammen mit den maßgefertigten Möbeln erhält das Interieur eine starke skandinavische Wurzel mit einem internationalen Touch.

Tel un bloc erratique niché dans une faille de la falaise, le bâtiment s'intègre parfaitement à son environnement. La force incessante de la nature a sculpté les roches, créant un refuge protégé des tempêtes de l'océan au sud-est. Avec le temps, la patine de la nature drainera également la couleur du bois, lui conférant les mêmes teintes argentées que les rochers environnants. Les saisons changeantes du paysage extérieur sont visibles dans chaque pièce, à travers de vastes surfaces vitrées et des vues soigneusement encadrées qui amènent la nature à l'intérieur. La proximité avec les vagues déchaînées procure, depuis l'intérieur, la sensation d'être en mer. Les couleurs et matériaux intérieurs ont été soigneusement sélectionnés pour créer une harmonie apaisante : briques du nord de la Suède, textiles en lin et bois de chêne. Avec du mobilier conçu sur mesure, l'intérieur ancre profondément ses racines scandinaves, tout en intégrant une touche internationale.

Como un bloque errático encajado en una grieta del acantilado, el edificio se integra con su entorno. La fuerza incesante de la naturaleza ha modelado las rocas, creando un refugio protegido de las tormentas del océano del sureste. Con el tiempo, también drenará los colores de la madera, dándole los mismos tonos plateados que las rocas circundantes. Las estaciones cambiantes del paisaje exterior están presentes en cada habitación, a través de grandes superficies acristaladas y vistas más pequeñas cuidadosamente enmarcadas que llevan la naturaleza al interior. La proximidad a las olas furiosas desde el interior da la sensación de estar en el mar. Los colores y materiales interiores han sido cuidadosamente seleccionados para crear una unidad tranquila: ladrillos del norte de Suecia, textiles de lino y madera de roble. Junto con los muebles diseñados a medida, el interior tiene una fuerte raíz escandinava con un toque internacional.

TRIGUEIROS ARCHITECTURE

ARCHITECTS' DIRECTORY >

P. 6

ARK-TELLUS

www.ark-tellus.no

Ark-Tellus was established in 2011 by Eivind Hanch-Hansen and Sverre Aaker Sondresen. The studio is located in Tønsberg, southwest of Oslo. Architects have broad experience with housing projects of all sizes. The work of the studio is based on a tectonic discussion of construction, materials and human scale, clarified from each particular site's topography and natural character. The dialogue between landscape and built environment and the desire to create a modern interpretation of local architecture, are consistent values.

Ark-Tellus wurde 2011 von Eivind Hanch-Hansen und Sverre Aaker Sondresen gegründet. Das Studio hat seinen Sitz in Tønsberg, südwestlich von Oslo. Die Architekten verfügen über umfassende Erfahrung in Wohnbauprojekten jeder Größe. Die Arbeit des Studios basiert auf einer tektonischen Auseinandersetzung mit Konstruktion, Materialien und menschlichem Maßstab, die sich aus der Topografie und dem natürlichen Charakter jedes spezifischen Standorts ableitet. Der Dialog zwischen Landschaft und gebauter Umgebung sowie der Wunsch, eine moderne Interpretation der lokalen Architektur zu schaffen, sind grundlegende Werte.

Ark-Tellus a été fondé en 2011 par Eivind Hanch-Hansen et Sverre Aaker Sondresen. L'atelier est situé à Tønsberg, au sud-ouest d'Oslo. Ses architectes possèdent une grande expérience dans la conception de logements de toutes tailles. Le travail du studio repose sur une réflexion tectonique autour de la construction, des matériaux et de l'échelle humaine, définie à partir de la topographie et du caractère naturel de chaque site spécifique. Le dialogue entre le paysage et l'environnement bâti, ainsi que le désir de proposer une interprétation moderne de l'architecture locale, sont des valeurs fondamentales.

Ark-Tellus fue fundada en 2011 por Eivind Hanch-Hansen y Sverre Aaker Sondresen. El estudio está ubicado en Tønsberg, al suroeste de Oslo. Sus arquitectos tienen una amplia experiencia en proyectos de vivienda de todos los tamaños. El trabajo del estudio se basa en una discusión tectónica sobre construcción, materiales y escala humana, definida a partir de la topografía y el carácter natural de cada sitio en particular. El diálogo entre el paisaje y el entorno construido, así como el deseo de crear una interpretación moderna de la arquitectura local, son valores fundamentales.

P. 24

ARKÍS ARCHITECTS

www.ark.is

ARKÍS Architects is a progressive design partnership practicing architecture, design, planning and green design consultancy. ARKÍS was founded in 1997, but from the firm's founding ARKÍS architects have executed projects at various scales and levels of complexity, both in Iceland and internationally, for institutional, private, and civic clients.
ARKÍS architects are driven by the pursuit of quality and the belief that the built environment has the inherent potential to improve the quality of our lives. Moreover, ARKÍS architects are committed to sustainable design practices. ARKÍS architects are the recipient of numerous awards and honors. Significant works include Holmen Aquatics Center, Holmsheidi Prison, the Icelandic Institute of Natural History, and Snaefellsstofa Visitor Center. The office of ARKÍS architects is located in Reykjavik, Iceland.

ARKÍS Architects ist ein Designverband, der Architektur, Design, Planung und ökologische Designberatung betreibt. Das Atelier wurde 1997 gegründet, hat aber seit seiner Gründung sowohl in Island als auch international Projekte unterschiedlichen Umfangs und unterschiedlicher Komplexität für institutionelle, private und öffentliche Auftraggeber durchgeführt.
Die Architekten von ARKIS werden von dem Streben nach Qualität und der Überzeugung angetrieben, dass die gebaute Umwelt das inhärente Potenzial hat, unsere Lebensqualität zu verbessern. Darüber hinaus haben sie sich zu nachhaltigen Gestaltungspraktiken verpflichtet.
ARKIS Architekten haben zahlreiche Auszeichnungen und Ehrungen erhalten. Zu ihren bedeutendsten Werken gehören das Holmen Aquatic Centre, das Holmsheidi-Gefängnis, das Isländische Institut für Naturgeschichte und das Besucherzentrum Snaefellsstofa. Das Architekturbüro ARKIS Architects hat seinen Sitz in Reykjavik, Island.

ARKÍS Architects est une association de design qui pratique l'architecture, le design, la planification et le conseil en design écologique. Le studio a été fondé en 1997, mais depuis sa création, il a réalisé des projets à différentes échelles et à différents niveaux de complexité, tant en Islande qu'à l'étranger, pour des clients institutionnels, privés et publics.
Les architectes d'ARKIS sont animés par la recherche de la qualité et la conviction que l'environnement bâti a le potentiel inhérent d'améliorer la qualité de notre vie. En outre, ils s'engagent à adopter des pratiques de conception durable. Les architectes d'ARKIS ont reçu de nombreux prix et distinctions. Parmi leurs oeuvres les plus importantes, on peut citer le centre aquatique de Holmen, la prison de Holmsheidi, l'Institut islandais d'histoire naturelle et le centre de visiteurs Snaefellsstofa. Le bureau ARKIS Architects est situé à Reykjavik, en Islande.

ARKÍS Architects es una asociación de diseño que practica la arquitectura, el diseño, la planificación y la consultoría de diseño ecológico. El estudio se fundó en 1997, pero desde su origen ha ejecutado proyectos en varias escalas y niveles de complejidad, tanto en Islandia como internacionalmente, para clientes institucionales, privados y públicos.
Los arquitectos de ARKÍS están impulsados por la búsqueda de la calidad y la creencia de que el entorno construido tiene el potencial inherente de mejorar la calidad de nuestras vidas. Además, están comprometidos con las prácticas de diseño sostenible. ARKÍS Architects han recibido numerosos premios y honores. Entre sus obras más significativas se incluyen el Centro Acuático de Holmen, la Prisión de Holmsheidi, el Instituto Islandés de Historia Natural y el Centro de Visitantes de Snaefellsstofa. El despacho de ARKIS Architects se encuentra en Reykjavik, Islandia.

P. 36

ARKITEKT MANUELA HARDY

www.mh-arkitektur.no

The half Swiss- half Norwegian architect started her own company late in 2017. She also has a background in interior design, and is keen on creating holistic architecture, working inside out, or outside in. Mainly working in the segment of detached houses and cottages, she always works closely together with her clients to achieve the best possible results. Another main method in her work, is to have an intuitive approach to every project. A well-designed home will result in feeling good for the habitants and their visitors. The outcome should always have character, function well in everyday life, as well as being unique at the same time. Therefore, it is important to treat every design process individually. Functionality, aesthetics and experience are key words in every project. The architecture should work as a backdrop or scenery, while the customer plays the main role in every home or project.

Die Architektin, mit schweizerisch-norwegischer Abstammung, gründete ihr eigenes Büro Ende 2017. Sie hat zudem eine Ausbildung im Bereich Innenarchitektur und konzentriert sich darauf, eine ganzheitliche Architektur zu schaffen, indem sie entweder von innen nach außen oder umgekehrt arbeitet. Ihr Schwerpunkt liegt auf Einfamilienhäusern und Ferienhäusern, wobei sie eng mit ihren Kunden zusammenarbeitet, um bestmögliche Ergebnisse zu erzielen. Ein weiterer zentraler Aspekt ihrer Arbeit ist ein intuitiver Ansatz in jedem Projekt. Ein gut gestaltetes Zuhause sollte sowohl seinen Bewohnern als auch seinen Besuchern ein Gefühl des Wohlbefindens vermitteln. Das Endergebnis sollte Charakter haben, im Alltag funktional sein und gleichzeitig einzigartig wirken. Deshalb ist es essenziell, jeden Gestaltungsprozess individuell zu betrachten. Funktionalität, Ästhetik und Erfahrung sind Schlüsselbegriffe in jedem ihrer Projekte. Architektur sollte als Kulisse oder Bühne fungieren, während der Kunde die Hauptrolle in jedem Zuhause oder Bauprojekt übernimmt.

L'architecte, d'origine suisse-norvégienne, a fondé sa propre entreprise fin 2017. Elle est également formée au design d'intérieur et se concentre sur une approche architecturale complète, travaillant de l'intérieur vers l'extérieur ou inversement. Elle se spécialise principalement dans les projets de maisons individuelles et de cabanes, collaborant étroitement avec ses clients pour obtenir les meilleurs résultats possibles. Une autre approche clé de son travail est d'adopter une démarche intuitive dans chaque projet. Une maison bien conçue doit procurer du bien-être à ses habitants et à ses visiteurs. Le résultat final doit avoir du caractère, être fonctionnel au quotidien et en même temps unique. C'est pourquoi chaque processus de conception doit être traité de manière individuelle. Fonctionnalité, esthétique et expérience sont des notions essentielles dans chacun de ses projets. L'architecture doit servir de toile de fond ou de scène, tandis que le client joue le rôle principal dans chaque maison ou projet.

La arquitecta, de ascendencia suizo-noruega, fundó su propia empresa a finales de 2017. También tiene formación en diseño de interiores y se enfoca en crear una arquitectura completa, trabajando desde el interior hacia el exterior o viceversa. Principalmente trabaja en proyectos de viviendas unifamiliares y cabañas, colaborando estrechamente con sus clientes para lograr los mejores resultados posibles. Otro método clave en su trabajo es adoptar un enfoque intuitivo en cada proyecto. Una vivienda bien diseñada debe generar bienestar tanto en sus habitantes como en sus visitantes. El resultado final debe tener carácter, funcionar bien en la vida cotidiana y, al mismo tiempo, ser único. Por ello, es fundamental tratar cada proceso de diseño de manera individual. Funcionalidad, estética y experiencia son palabras clave en cada proyecto. La arquitectura debe funcionar como un telón de fondo o escenario, mientras que el cliente ocupa el papel principal en cada hogar o proyecto.

P. 44

ASAS ARKITEKTUR

www.as-as.no

ASAS is a well established architecture office founded in 1980 and based in three different locations in Norway. Typical building typologies are health care buildings, housing, school, kindergartens and offices, in both private and public sectors. We consist of 19 architects, interior designers, urbanists and graphic designers in a nonhierarchical system with a social profile. We have a strong reputation as a versatile, playful and tidy architecture office. Our mantra is precision at all levels. We always promise ourselves and our clients to deliver solid and innovative projects. Hand sketching is supplied by testing spatial qualities in physical models before the projects enter the 3D digital world. This gives our team time to investigate the optimal relation between form, space and function, and to choose the correct strategy for sustainability, systems and materials.

ASAS ist ein Architekturbüro, das 1980 gegründet wurde und an drei verschiedenen Standorten in Norwegen tätig ist. Häufige Gebäudetypologien umfassen Gesundheitseinrichtungen, Wohnhäuser, Schulen, Kindergärten und Büros – sowohl im öffentlichen als auch im privaten Sektor. Unser Team besteht aus 19 Architekten, Innenarchitekten, Stadtplanern und Grafikdesignern, die in einem nicht-hierarchischen System mit sozialem Profil organisiert sind. Wir genießen einen soliden Ruf als vielseitiges, kreatives und akribisches Architekturbüro. Unser Mantra ist Präzision auf allen Ebenen. Wir verpflichten uns selbst und unsere Kunden, solide und innovative Projekte zu liefern. Die handgezeichneten Skizzen werden durch räumliche Modellstudien ergänzt, bevor sie in eine digitale 3D-Umgebung überführt werden. Dies ermöglicht es uns, die optimale Beziehung zwischen Form, Raum und Funktion zu erforschen und die beste Strategie in Bezug auf Nachhaltigkeit, Systeme und Materialien zu wählen.

ASAS est un cabinet d'architecture fondé en 1980 et implanté dans trois localisations différentes en Norvège. Nous réalisons divers types de bâtiments, notamment des établissements de santé, des logements, des écoles, des crèches et des bureaux, tant dans le secteur public que privé. Nous comptons une équipe de 19 architectes, designers d'intérieur, urbanistes et graphistes, organisée selon un système non hiérarchique et axée sur le social. Nous jouissons d'une solide réputation en tant qu'agence d'architecture polyvalente, créative et rigoureuse. Notre mantra est la précision à tous les niveaux. Nous nous engageons auprès de nous-mêmes et de nos clients à livrer des projets solides et innovants. Les croquis manuels sont complétés par des maquettes physiques pour tester les qualités spatiales avant de passer à la modélisation numérique en 3D. Cette méthodologie nous permet d'explorer l'interaction optimale entre forme, espace et fonction, et de choisir la meilleure stratégie en termes de durabilité, de systèmes et de matériaux.

ASAS es una oficina de arquitectura fundada en 1980 y con sede en tres ubicaciones diferentes de Noruega. Tipologías comunes de edificios incluyen instalaciones de salud, viviendas, escuelas, guarderías y oficinas, tanto en el sector público como privado. Contamos con un equipo de 19 arquitectos, diseñadores de interiores, urbanistas y diseñadores gráficos, organizados en un sistema no jerárquico con un perfil social. Tenemos una sólida reputación como un estudio de arquitectura versátil, creativo y meticuloso. Nuestro mantra es la precisión en todos los niveles. Nos comprometemos con nosotros mismos y con nuestros clientes a entregar proyectos sólidos e innovadores. Los bocetos manuales se complementan con pruebas de cualidades espaciales en modelos físicos antes de pasar al entorno digital en 3D. Esto nos permite investigar la relación óptima entre forma, espacio y función, y elegir la mejor estrategia en términos de sostenibilidad, sistemas y materiales.

P. 56

DELIN ARKITEKTKONTOR

www.delinarkitektkontor.se

Buster, borned 1967, was educated at Beckmans School of Design in Stockholm, where he now teaches architecture and interior design. He has broad experience of design in many different fields, from graphic design, industrial design, furniture design, exhibitions, offices, shops, restaurants and commissions for private clients such as kitchens, bathrooms, holiday homes and villas.
He has been active since 1997 and has extensive experience in construction engineering and and how to implement advanced projects together with a well-established network of contractors. As a client, you can trust that Buster is dedicated and meticulous and performs all tasks with utmost dedication.

Buster, geboren 1967, wurde an der Beckmans School of Design in Stockholm ausgebildet, wo er heute Architektur und Innendesign lehrt. Er verfügt über umfassende Erfahrung mit Design in vielen verschiedenen Bereichen, von Grafikdesign, Industriedesign, Möbeldesign, Ausstellungen, Büros, Geschäften, Restaurants und Aufträgen für private Auftraggeber wie Küchen, Bäder, Ferienhäuser und Villen.
Er ist seit 1997 tätig und verfügt über umfassende Erfahrung im Bauingenieurwesen und in der Umsetzung fortgeschrittener Projekte zusammen mit einem gut etablierten Netzwerk von Auftragnehmern. Als Kunde können Sie darauf vertrauen, dass Buster engagiert und akribisch ist und alle Aufgaben mit größter Hingabe ausführt.

Buster, né en 1967, a fait ses études à l'école de design Beckmans à Stockholm, où il enseigne aujourd'hui l'architecture et le design d'intérieur. Il a une grande expérience du design dans de nombreux domaines, du graphisme au design industriel, en passant par la conception de meubles, les expositions, les bureaux, les magasins, les restaurants et les commandes pour des clients privés comme les cuisines, les salles de bains, les maisons de vacances et les villas.
Il est actif depuis 1997 et possède une vaste expérience de l'ingénierie de la construction et de la mise en oeuvre de projets avancés en collaboration avec un réseau d'entrepreneurs bien établi. En tant que client, vous pouvez être sûr que Buster est dévoué et méticuleux et qu'il accomplit toutes les tâches avec le plus grand dévouement.

Buster, nacido en 1967, se educó en la Escuela de Diseño de Beckmans en Estocolmo, donde ahora enseña arquitectura y diseño de interiores. Tiene una amplia experiencia en diseño en muchos campos diferentes, desde diseño gráfico, diseño industrial, diseño de muebles, exposiciones, oficinas, tiendas, restaurantes y encargos para clientes privados como cocinas, baños, casas de vacaciones y villas.
Ha estado activo desde 1997 y tiene una amplia experiencia en la ingeniería de construcción y en cómo implementar proyectos avanzados junto con una red bien establecida de contratistas. Como cliente, puede confiar en que Buster es dedicado y meticuloso y realiza todas las tareas con la máxima dedicación.

P. 62

ERLING BERG

www.erlingberg.com

Norwegian born, Erling Berg is an architect and designer with a passion for crafting unique spaces addressing the important relationship between scale, form, light and the use of genuine materials, carefully considering context and functionality. With a rigorous and concept-driven approach, Berg focuses on timeless aesthetics, delicate details and simplicity within the built environment. Berg, who spent the majority of his twenties and his early thirties in California finds inspiration in the horizontal language of mid-century architecture from the region, as well as the Norwegian vernacular and its long building traditions, focusing on wood as the main structural, exterior and interior component. From his studio in Fredrikstad, Norway – Berg continues to to create one of a kind dwellings that often are set in rural surroundings, on sloped and challenging terrain and in touch with nature.

Geboren in Norwegen, ist Erling Berg ein Architekt und Designer mit einer Leidenschaft für die Schaffung einzigartiger Räume, die die wichtige Beziehung zwischen Maßstab, Form, Licht und der Verwendung von authentischen Materialien ansprechen, wobei der Kontext und die Funktionalität sorgfältig berücksichtigt werden. Mit einem rigorosen und konzeptbasierten Ansatz konzentriert sich Berg auf zeitlose Ästhetik, feine Details und Einfachheit in der gebauten Umgebung. Berg, der den Großteil seiner Zwanziger und frühen Dreißigerjahre in Kalifornien verbracht hat, findet Inspiration in der horizontalen Sprache der Architektur der Mitte des 20. Jahrhunderts in der Region sowie im norwegischen Volksmund und seinen langen Bautraditionen, wobei Holz als Hauptstrukturkomponente sowohl im Außen- als auch im Innenbereich im Mittelpunkt steht. Von seinem Studio in Fredrikstad, Norwegen, aus setzt Berg seine Arbeit fort und entwirft oft einzigartige Wohnhäuser, die sich häufig in ländlichen Umgebungen auf schwierigen, geneigten Grundstücken befinden und immer im Kontakt mit der Natur stehen.

Né en Norvège, Erling Berg est un architecte et designer passionné par la création d'espaces uniques qui explorent la relation importante entre l'échelle, la forme, la lumière et l'utilisation de matériaux authentiques, en tenant compte attentivement du contexte et de la fonctionnalité. Avec une approche rigoureuse et conceptuelle, Berg se concentre sur des esthétiques intemporelles, des détails délicats et la simplicité dans l'environnement bâti. Ayant passé la majeure partie de ses vingtaine et du début de ses trente ans en Californie, Berg trouve son inspiration dans le langage horizontal de l'architecture du milieu du XXe siècle de la région, ainsi que dans le vernaculaire norvégien et ses longues traditions de construction, mettant l'accent sur le bois comme composant structurel principal, tant à l'extérieur qu'à l'intérieur. Depuis son studio à Fredrikstad, en Norvège, Berg continue de créer des logements uniques qui sont souvent situés dans des environnements ruraux, sur des terrains pentus et difficiles, toujours en contact avec la nature.

Nacido en Noruega, Erling Berg es un arquitecto y diseñador con una pasión por crear espacios únicos que aborden la importante relación entre la escala, la forma, la luz y el uso de materiales genuinos, considerando cuidadosamente el contexto y la funcionalidad. Con un enfoque riguroso y basado en conceptos, Berg se centra en estéticas atemporales, detalles delicados y simplicidad dentro del entorno construido. Berg, quien pasó la mayor parte de sus veinte años y principios de sus treinta en California, encuentra inspiración en el lenguaje horizontal de la arquitectura de mediados del siglo XX de la región, así como en el vernáculo noruego y sus largas tradiciones de construcción, centrándose en la madera como componente estructural principal, tanto exterior como interior. Desde su estudio en Fredrikstad, Noruega, Berg continúa creando viviendas únicas que a menudo se ubican en entornos rurales, en terrenos inclinados y desafiantes, siempre en contacto con la naturaleza.

P. 72

FJORD ARKITEKTER

www.fjordarkitekter.no

Fjord Arkitekter designs sustainable, functional, and aesthetic architecture. Their approach integrates efficient materials, mindful design, and minimal environmental impact. Inspired by history and landscape, they create spaces with identity and a sense of belonging. They prioritize well-being, social interaction, and long-lasting solutions, favoring transformation over demolition. Thoughtful financial planning ensures project feasibility. Beyond function, they emphasize architecture's spiritual dimension, crafting spaces that inspire contemplation through light, proportion, and materiality.

Fjord Arkitekter entwirft nachhaltige, funktionale und ästhetische Architektur. Ihr Ansatz integriert effiziente Materialien, durchdachtes Design und minimalen Umweltimpact. Inspiriert von Geschichte und Landschaft, schaffen sie Räume mit Identität und Zugehörigkeitsgefühl. Sie priorisieren Wohlbefinden, soziale Interaktion und langlebige Lösungen, wobei sie Transformation der Abriss bevorzugen. Sorgfältige finanzielle Planung sichert die Machbarkeit der Projekte. Über die Funktion hinaus betonen sie die spirituelle Dimension der Architektur und gestalten Räume, die durch Licht, Proportion und Materialität zur Kontemplation einladen.

Fjord Arkitekter conçoit une architecture durable, fonctionnelle et esthétique. Leur approche intègre des matériaux efficaces, un design réfléchi et un impact environnemental minimal. Inspirés par l'histoire et le paysage, ils créent des espaces avec identité et sentiment d'appartenance. Ils privilégient le bien-être, l'interaction sociale et des solutions durables, favorisant la transformation plutôt que la démolition. Une planification financière rigoureuse garantit la faisabilité des projets. Au-delà de la fonction, ils soulignent la dimension spirituelle de l'architecture, créant des espaces qui inspirent la contemplation à travers la lumière, la proportion et la matérialité.

Fjord Arkitekter crea arquitectura sostenible, funcional y estética. Su enfoque integra materiales eficientes, diseño consciente y un mínimo impacto ambiental. Inspirados en la historia y el paisaje, buscan generar espacios con identidad y sentido de pertenencia. Promueven el bienestar y la interacción social, priorizando soluciones duraderas y transformables sobre la demolición. La planificación económica es clave en sus proyectos, garantizando viabilidad financiera. Más allá de la funcionalidad, enfatizan la dimensión espiritual de la arquitectura, creando espacios que invitan a la contemplación a través de la luz, la proporción y la materialidad.

P. 82

GOA ARKITEKTKONTOR

www.goaark.no

GOA Arkitektkontor was founded in 2012 by Johannes Goa Ludvigsen with an ambition to create simple and straightforward architecture routed in the Scandinavian building tradition. A thorough understanding of local context is key to our approach, as we strive to create dynamic architecture rich in its dialogue with site and natural surroundings. Our work combines the use of natural materials and traditional construction techniques with a contemporary architectural language. During execution, we hone in on critical detailing within an economy of means, thereby giving our projects a minimal, delicate, precise and often subtly underplayed identity.

GOA Arkitektkontor wurde 2012 von Johannes Goa Ludvigsen mit der Ambition gegründet, eine einfache und direkte Architektur zu schaffen, die in der skandinavischen Bautradition verwurzelt ist. Ein tiefes Verständnis des lokalen Kontexts ist ein zentraler Bestandteil unseres Ansatzes, da wir eine dynamische Architektur anstreben, die mit ihrer Umgebung und der Natur im Dialog steht. Unsere Arbeit verbindet den Einsatz natürlicher Materialien und traditioneller Bautechniken mit einer zeitgenössischen architektonischen Sprache. Während der Umsetzung legen wir großen Wert auf wesentliche Details innerhalb einer ökonomischen Mittelverwendung, um Projekte mit einer minimalistischen, feinen, präzisen und subtil ausdrucksstarken Identität zu realisieren.

GOA Arkitektkontor a été fondé en 2012 par Johannes Goa Ludvigsen avec l'ambition de créer une architecture simple et directe, enracinée dans la tradition constructive scandinave. Une compréhension approfondie du contexte local est essentielle à notre approche, car nous cherchons à développer une architecture dynamique en dialogue avec son environnement et la nature. Notre travail associe l'utilisation de matériaux naturels et de techniques de construction traditionnelles à un langage architectural contemporain. Lors de l'exécution, nous nous concentrons sur les détails essentiels avec une économie de moyens, réalisant des projets à l'identité minimaliste, délicate, précise et subtilement expressive.

GOA Arkitektkontor fue fundada en 2012 por Johannes Goa Ludvigsen con la ambición de crear una arquitectura simple y directa, enraizada en la tradición constructiva escandinava. Una comprensión profunda del contexto local es clave en nuestro enfoque, ya que buscamos crear una arquitectura dinámica en diálogo con el entorno y la naturaleza. Nuestro trabajo combina el uso de materiales naturales y técnicas de construcción tradicionales con un lenguaje arquitectónico contemporáneo. Durante la ejecución, nos enfocamos en los detalles esenciales dentro de una economía de medios, logrando proyectos con una identidad minimalista, delicada, precisa y sutilmente expresiva.

P. 94

GUDMUNDUR JONSSON ARKITEKTKONTOR

www.gudmundurjonsson.no

Gudmundur Jonsson Arkitektkontor was established in 1987 in Oslo. Ever since they have won 37 different prizes in Norwegian, Icelandic and Nordic competitions, some of them 1st and 2nd prizes. The essence of "reading the site" has been of utmost importance and the emphasis of the dialog between nature and the house. Construction and materiality is supposed to clarify the concept, and the heritage of functionalism is often an inspiration in the projects. Definition of volumes are often made more distinctive by the cantilevered roofs and balconies, simultaneously defining the spaces and giving excitement and dialog between the building and the landscape. An extensive use of glass is strengthening the constructive challenges. In the interior the purpose is to make surfaces appear as a softening unity, integrating closets, cabinets and technical installations to obtain maximum harmony and tranquility, enforced by the colour-palette.

Das Gudmundur Jonsson Arkitektkontor wurde 1987 in Oslo gegründet. Seitdem hat es 37 verschiedene Preise in norwegischen, isländischen und weiteren nordischen Wettbewerben gewonnen, darunter erste und zweite Preise. Die Essenz des „Lesens des Ortes" war von größter Bedeutung, sowie die Betonung des Dialogs zwischen Natur und Haus. Konstruktion und Materialität sollen das Konzept verdeutlichen, und das Erbe des Funktionalismus ist oft eine Inspiration in den Projekten. Die Definition der Volumina wird oft durch die auskragenden Dächer und Balkone verstärkt, die gleichzeitig die Räume definieren und für Spannung und Dialog zwischen dem Gebäude und der Landschaft sorgen. Ein umfangreicher Einsatz von Glas verstärkt die konstruktiven Herausforderungen. Im Inneren sollen die Oberflächen als eine weichmachende Einheit erscheinen, indem Schränke, Vitrinen und technische Installationen integriert werden, um ein Maximum an Harmonie und Ruhe zu erreichen, die durch die Farbpalette verstärkt wird.

Gudmundur Jonsson Arkitektkontor a été créé en 1987 à Oslo. Depuis, ils ont remporté 37 prix différents dans des concours norvégiens, islandais et nordiques, dont certains 1er et 2e prix. L'essence de la « lecture du site » a été de la plus haute importance et l'accent a été mis sur le dialogue entre la nature et la maison. La construction et la matérialité sont censées clarifier le concept et l'héritage du fonctionnalisme est souvent une source d'inspiration dans les projets. Les toits et les balcons en porte-à-faux permettent de définir des volumes de manière plus distinctive. Ils définissent simultanément les espaces et donnent de l'animation et du dialogue entre le bâtiment et le paysage. L'utilisation intensive du verre renforce les défis de construction. À l'intérieur, l'objectif est de faire apparaître les surfaces comme une unité adoucissante, en intégrant les placards, les armoires et les installations techniques pour obtenir une harmonie et une tranquillité maximales, renforcées par la palette de couleurs.

Gudmundur Jonsson Arkitektkontor se estableció en 1987 en Oslo. Desde entonces han ganado 37 premios en competiciones noruegas, islandesas y nórdicas, algunos de ellos el primer y segundo premio. La lectura e interpretación del lugar es de suma importancia en sus proyectos, así como el énfasis del diálogo entre la naturaleza y la casa. Se supone que la construcción y la materialidad aclaran el concepto, y por ello, la herencia del funcionalismo se convierte a menudo en su fuente de inspiración. La definición de los volúmenes se distingue por los tejados en voladizo y los balcones, delimitando simultáneamente los espacios y dando emoción y diálogo entre edificio y paisaje. El uso extensivo del vidrio refuerza estos desafíos. En el interior, el propósito es hacer que las superficies aparezcan en suave unidad, integrando armarios e instalaciones técnicas para obtener la máxima armonía y tranquilidad, reforzadas por una elegante paleta de colores.

P. 114

JAN HENRIK JANSEN ARKITEKTER

www.janhenrikjansen.dk

Jan Henrik Jansen is a Danish/German architect based in Copenhagen, Denmark. He holds degrees from Leibniz Universität, Hannover and Aarhus School of Architecture and has taught at the University of applied science in Lübeck, Germany and DIS in Copenhagen.
Between 2002 and 2016 Jansen designed and single-handedly built three distinctive, award winning summer houses, "Langelinie", "Black+Bright" and "Birkedal", on the Danish island of Møn. These three houses served as a laboratory where Jansen experimented with design, details and materials and led to the launch of his practice, Jan Henrik Jansen arkitekter, in 2012. Jansen now works internationally, designing quietly radical, materially-rich and geometrically precise houses that are highly sensitive to the diverse landscapes that they occupy.

Jan Henrik Jansen ist ein dänisch-deutscher Architekt mit Sitz in Kopenhagen, Dänemark. Er hat Abschlüsse der Leibniz-Universität, Hannover und der Aarhus School of Architecture und lehrte an der Fachhochschule Lübeck, Deutschland, und der DIS in Kopenhagen.
Zwischen 2002 und 2016 entwarf und baute Jansen eigenhändig drei unverwechselbare, preisgekrönte Sommerhäuser, „Langelinie", „Black+Bright" und „Birkedal", auf der dänischen Insel Møn. Diese drei Häuser dienten als Laboratorium, in dem Jansen mit Design, Details und Materialien experimentierte, und führten zur Gründung seines Büros Jan Henrik Jansen arkitekter im Jahr 2012. Heute arbeitet Jansen international und entwirft leise, radikale, materialreiche und geometrisch präzise Häuser, die sehr sensibel auf die vielfältigen Landschaften reagieren, die sie besetzen.

Jan Henrik Jansen est un architecte danois-allemand basé à Copenhague, au Danemark. Il est diplômé de l'université Leibniz, de Hanovre et de l'école d'architecture d'Aarhus. Il a enseigné à l'université des sciences appliquées de Lübeck, en Allemagne et à la DIS de Copenhague.
Entre 2002 et 2016, Jansen a conçu et construit à lui seul trois maisons d'été distinctes et primées : « Langelinie », « Black+Bright » et « Birkedal », sur l'île danoise de Møn. Ces trois maisons ont servi de laboratoire où Jansen a expérimenté le design, les détails et les matériaux et ont conduit au lancement de sa pratique, Jan Henrik Jansen arkitekter, en 2012. Jansen travaille maintenant à l'échelle internationale, concevant des maisons discrètement radicales, riches en matériaux et géométriquement précises, très sensibles aux divers paysages qu'elles occupent.

Jan Henrik Jansen es un arquitecto danés/alemán con sede en Copenhague, Dinamarca. Tiene títulos de la Leibniz Universität, Hannover y la Escuela de Arquitectura de Aarhus y ha enseñado en la Universidad de Ciencias Aplicadas de Lübeck, Alemania y en la DIS de Copenhague.
Entre 2002 y 2016, Jansen diseñó y construyó por su cuenta tres casas de verano distintivas y premiadas, «Langelinie», «Black+Bright» y «Birkedal », en la isla danesa de Møn. Estas tres casas sirvieron como un laboratorio donde Jansen experimentó con el diseño, los detalles y los materiales y condujo al lanzamiento de su estudio, Jan Henrik Jansen arkitekter, en 2012. Jansen trabaja ahora internacionalmente, diseñando casas silenciosamente radicales, ricas en materiales y geométricamente precisas que son altamente sensibles a los diversos paisajes que ocupan.

P. 132

KAMINSKY ARKITEKTUR

www.kaminsky.se

Kaminsky Arkitektur is an award-winning firm founded in 2007 with 60 employees in offices in Gothenburg and Stockholm. The firm is dedicated to developing cutting-edge architecture and has positioned itself as an international benchmark for sustainable architecture and an active voice in contemporary debate. Established in 2007 by Fredrik Kjellgren and Joakim Kaminsky as Kjellgren Kaminsky Arkitekter, the firm transitioned in 2021 when Fredrik departed. Today, Joakim Kaminsky continues the legacy leading the office.
Joakim Kaminsky has been awarded several prestigious scholarships, brings his expertise from roles at UN-Studio and Wingårdhs. He regularly teaches at Chalmers Architecture and has been a guest lecturer at architecture schools in Stockholm, Lund, Århus, and Trondheim.

Kaminsky Arkitektur ist ein preisgekröntes Unternehmen, das 2007 gegründet wurde und 60 Mitarbeiter in Büros in Göteborg und Stockholm beschäftigt. Das Büro widmet sich der Entwicklung modernster Architektur und hat sich als internationaler Maßstab für nachhaltige Architektur und als aktive Stimme in der zeitgenössischen Debatte positioniert. Das Büro wurde 2007 von Fredrik Kjellgren und Joakim Kaminsky als Kjellgren Kaminsky Arkitekter gegründet und 2021 nach dem Ausscheiden von Fredrik Kaminsky umgewandelt. Heute führt Joakim Kaminsky das Erbe fort und leitet das Büro.
Joakim Kaminsky wurde mit mehreren renommierten Stipendien ausgezeichnet und bringt sein Fachwissen aus seiner Tätigkeit bei UN-Studio und Wingårdhs mit. Er unterrichtet regelmäßig an der Chalmers Architecture und war Gastdozent an Architekturschulen in Stockholm, Lund, Århus und Trondheim.

Kaminsky Arkitektur est un cabinet primé fondé en 2007 avec 60 employés répartis dans des bureaux à Göteborg et Stockholm. Le cabinet est dédié au développement d'une architecture de pointe et s'est positionné comme une référence internationale en matière d'architecture durable et comme une voix active dans le débat contemporain. Établi en 2007 par Fredrik Kjellgren et Joakim Kaminsky en tant que Kjellgren Kaminsky Arkitekter, le cabinet a fait la transition en 2021 lorsque Fredrik est parti. Aujourd'hui, Joakim Kaminsky perpétue l'héritage en dirigeant le cabinet.
Joakim Kaminsky a reçu plusieurs bourses prestigieuses, apportant son expertise acquise chez UN-Studio et Wingårdhs. Il enseigne régulièrement à la Chalmers Architecture et a été conférencier invité dans des écoles d'architecture à Stockholm, Lund, Århus et Trondheim.

Kaminsky Arkitektur es una galardonada empresa fundada en 2007 con 60 empleados que trabajan en oficinas en Gotemburgo y Estocolmo. La firma se dedica a desarrollar arquitectura de vanguardia y se ha posicionado como un referente internacional de la arquitectura sostenible y una voz activa en el debate contemporáneo. Fundada en 2007 por Fredrik Kjellgren y Joakim Kaminsky con el nombre de Kjellgren Kaminsky Arkitekter, la empresa pasó a llamarse Kjellgren Kaminsky Arkitekter en 2021, cuando Fredrik se marchó. Hoy, Joakim Kaminsky continúa el legado al frente del despacho.
Joakim Kaminsky ha recibido varias becas de prestigio y aporta su experiencia en UN-Studio y Wingårdhs. Imparte clases regularmente en Chalmers Architecture y ha sido profesor invitado en escuelas de arquitectura de Estocolmo, Lund, Århus y Trondheim.

KNUT HJELTNES

www.hjeltnes.as

Knut Hjeltnes was born in Drøbak, Norway in 1961, and was raised in Ås, a small university town south of Oslo. He studied at the Norwegian Institute of Technology in Trondheim from 1980 -1986. During the latter half of his studies and for one and a half years after graduating he worked for 4B Architects. Since 1988 he has had his on practice. He taught at the Oslo school of Architecture from 1988-2016, the last 12 years as professor. He has lectured in several countries, been awarded several prizes and his work is widely published. The practice was established in Oslo as a one-man practice, slowly expanding to its current size of six employees. The office concentrate on houses, weekend homes and smaller public works. In a period over several years in the 1990s he cooperated with Haga and Grov Architects in Stavanger.

Knut Hjeltnes wurde 1961 in Drøbak, Norwegen, geboren und wuchs in Ås, einer kleinen Universitätsstadt südlich von Oslo, auf. Er studierte von 1980 bis 1986 am Norwegischen Institut für Technologie in Trondheim. Während der zweiten Hälfte seines Studiums und eineinhalb Jahre nach seinem Abschluss arbeitete er für 4B Architects. Seit 1988 hat er sein eigenes Büro. Von 1988 bis 2016 unterrichtete er an der Oslo School of Architecture, die letzten 12 Jahre als Professor. Er hat in mehreren Ländern Vorlesungen gehalten, wurde mit mehreren Preisen ausgezeichnet, und seine Arbeiten werden vielfach veröffentlicht. Das Büro wurde in Oslo als Ein-Mann-Praxis gegründet, die sich langsam auf ihre derzeitige Größe von sechs Mitarbeitern ausweitete. Das Büro konzentriert sich auf Häuser, Wochenendhäuser und kleinere öffentliche Arbeiten. In den 1990er Jahren arbeitete er über mehrere Jahre hinweg mit Haga and Grov Architects in Stavanger zusammen.

Knut Hjeltnes est né à Drøbak, en Norvège, en 1961, et a grandi à Ås, une petite ville universitaire au sud d'Oslo. Il a étudié à l'Institut norvégien de technologie de Trondheim de 1980 à 1986. Pendant la seconde moitié de ses études et pendant un an et demi après l'obtention de son diplôme, il a travaillé pour 4B Architects. Depuis 1988, il a son propre cabinet. Il a enseigné à l'école d'architecture d'Oslo de 1988 à 2016, les 12 dernières années en tant que professeur. Il a donné des conférences dans plusieurs pays, a reçu plusieurs prix et ses travaux sont largement publiés. Le cabinet a été créé à Oslo en tant que cabinet unipersonnel et s'est lentement développé pour atteindre sa taille actuelle de six employés. Le bureau se concentre sur les maisons, les résidences secondaires et les petits travaux publics. Dans les années 1990, il a coopéré pendant plusieurs années avec Haga and Grov Architects à Stavanger.

Knut Hjeltnes nació en Drøbak, Noruega, en 1961, y se crió en Ås, una pequeña ciudad universitaria al sur de Oslo. Estudió en el Instituto Noruego de Tecnología en Trondheim de 1980 a 1986. Durante la última mitad de sus estudios y durante un año y medio después de graduarse trabajó para 4B Architects. Desde 1988 ha tenido su propio estudio. Enseñó en la Escuela de Arquitectura de Oslo de 1988 a 2016, los últimos 12 años como profesor. Ha dado conferencias en varios países, ha recibido varios premios y su trabajo es ampliamente publicado. El estudio se estableció en Oslo como un estudio de un solo hombre, expandiéndose lentamente hasta su tamaño actual de seis empleados. La oficina se concentra en el diseño de casas, casas de fin de semana y pequeñas obras públicas. En un período de varios años en la década de 1990 cooperó con Haga and Grov Architects en Stavanger.

P. 160

KOLMAN BOYE

www.kolmanboye.se

Founded in 2013 by Erik Kolman Janouch and Victor Boye Julebäk, Kolman Boye Architects integrates research and practice, investigating materials and techniques with sensitivity to experience, heritage, and materiality. Their approach fosters beauty, sustainability, and a dialogue between architecture and context. Victor Boye, PhD in architecture, teaches at the Royal Danish Academy, while Erik Kolman, architect, runs a small construction company, reinforcing the link between design and craftsmanship.

Gegründet 2013 von Erik Kolman Janouch und Victor Boye Julebäk, verbindet Kolman Boye Architects Forschung und Praxis, untersucht Materialien und Techniken mit Sensibilität für Erfahrung, Erbe und Materialität. Ihr Ansatz fördert Schönheit, Nachhaltigkeit und einen Dialog zwischen Architektur und Kontext. Victor Boye, promovierter Architekt, lehrt an der Royal Danish Academy, während Erik Kolman, Architekt, eine kleine Baufirma leitet und so die Verbindung zwischen Design und Handwerk stärkt.

Fondé en 2013 par Erik Kolman Janouch et Victor Boye Julebäk, Kolman Boye Architects allie recherche et pratique, explorant les matériaux et techniques avec une sensibilité à l'expérience, au patrimoine et à la matérialité. Leur approche favorise la beauté, la durabilité et un dialogue entre l'architecture et son contexte. Victor Boye, docteur en architecture, enseigne à la Royal Danish Academy, tandis qu'Erik Kolman, architecte, dirige une petite entreprise de construction, renforçant le lien entre conception et artisanat.

Fundado en 2013 por Erik Kolman Janouch y Victor Boye Julebäk, Kolman Boye Architects integra investigación y práctica, explorando materiales y técnicas con sensibilidad hacia la experiencia, la herencia cultural y la materialidad. Su enfoque fomenta la belleza, la sostenibilidad y el diálogo entre la arquitectura y su contexto. Victor Boye, doctor en arquitectura, enseña en la Royal Danish Academy, mientras que Erik Kolman, arquitecto, dirige una pequeña empresa de construcción, reforzando el vínculo entre diseño y artesanía.

P. 182

MARGE ARKITEKTER

www.marge.se

Marge Arkitekter was established in 2002 by Pye Aurell Ehrström, Katarina Grundsell, Louise Masreliez and Susanne Ramel. The firm rapidly became recognised as one of the young firms representing a contemporary development of architecture in Sweden and today has an extensive portfolio including private, commercial and public projects. Marge Arkitekter has received publicity in the national and international press and has exhibited in Sweden and around Europe. The firm currently has 36 employees. Marge Arkitekter works in architecture on every scale, from town planning to interior fittings and product design. Common to the projects is a spatially exploratory architecture that is characterised by innovative organization and new applications for materials.

Marge Arkitekter wurde 2002 von Pye Aurell Ehrström, Katarina Grundsell, Louise Masreliez und Susanne Ramel gegründet. Das Büro wurde schnell als eines der jungen Büros anerkannt, die für eine zeitgenössische Entwicklung der Architektur in Schweden stehen, und verfügt heute über ein umfangreiches Portfolio, das private, gewerbliche und öffentliche Projekte umfasst. Marge Arkitekter wurde in der nationalen und internationalen Presse bekannt gemacht und hat in Schweden und in ganz Europa ausgestellt. Das Büro hat derzeit 36 Mitarbeiter. Marge Arkitekter arbeitet in der Architektur in jeder Größenordnung, von der Stadtplanung bis zur Innenausstattung und zum Produktdesign. Gemeinsam ist den Projekten eine räumlich explorative Architektur, die sich durch innovative Organisation und neue Materialanwendungen auszeichnet.

Marge Arkitekter a été créée en 2002 par Pye Aurell Ehrström, Katarina Grundsell, Louise Masreliez et Susanne Ramel. Le cabinet a rapidement été reconnu comme l'un des jeunes cabinets représentant un développement contemporain de l'architecture en Suède et possède aujourd'hui un vaste portefeuille comprenant des projets privés, commerciaux et publics. Marge Arkitekter a fait l'objet d'une publicité dans la presse nationale et internationale et a exposé en Suède et dans toute l'Europe. La société compte actuellement 36 employés. Marge Arkitekter travaille dans le domaine de l'architecture à toutes les échelles, de l'urbanisme à l'aménagement intérieur et à la conception de produits. Les projets ont en commun une architecture exploratoire dans l'espace qui se caractérise par une organisation innovante et de nouvelles applications des matériaux.

Marge Arkitekter fue fundada en 2002 por Pye Aurell Ehrström, Katarina Grundsell, Louise Masreliez y Susanne Ramel. La empresa se convirtió rápidamente en una de las jóvenes firmas que representan un desarrollo contemporáneo de la arquitectura en Suecia y hoy en día tiene una amplia cartera que incluye proyectos privados, comerciales y públicos. Marge Arkitekter ha recibido publicidad en la prensa nacional e internacional y ha expuesto en Suecia y en toda Europa. La empresa tiene actualmente 36 empleados. Marge Arkitekter trabaja en la arquitectura a todas las escalas, desde el urbanismo hasta el equipamiento interior y el diseño de productos. Lo común en sus proyectos es una arquitectura de exploración espacial que se caracteriza por una organización innovadora y nuevas aplicaciones de materiales.

P.190

MARGEN WIGOW ARKITEKTKONTOR

www.margenwigow.se

Margen Wigow Arkitektkontor AB was started in 2000 and is run by Cecilia Margen Wigow architect SAR / MSA. The office specializes in new and refurbished villas and holiday homes. We are driven by job satisfaction and a genuine interest in architecture. The aim is to create environments of high architectural value based on the client's wishes, the conditions of the site and the project budget. The ambition is to follow all the stages of the project from sketch to building follow-up in order to implement the architectural ideas down to the detail level.

Margen Wigow Arkitektkontor AB wurde im Jahr 2000 gegründet und wird von Cecilia Margen Wigow, Architektin SAR / MSA, geleitet. Das Büro ist auf neue und renovierte Villen und Ferienhäuser spezialisiert. Unser Antrieb sind Arbeitszufriedenheit und ein echtes Interesse an Architektur. Ziel ist es, Umgebungen von hohem architektonischem Wert zu schaffen, basierend auf den Wünschen des Kunden, den Bedingungen des Standortes und dem Projektbudget. Es wird angestrebt, alle Phasen des Projekts von der Skizze bis zur Bauausführung zu verfolgen, um die architektonischen Ideen bis ins Detail umzusetzen.

Margen Wigow Arkitektkontor AB a été créée en 2000 et est dirigée par Cecilia Margen Wigow architecte SAR / MSA. Le bureau est spécialisé dans les villas et maisons de vacances neuves et rénovées. Nous sommes motivés par la satisfaction professionnelle et un véritable intérêt pour l'architecture. L'objectif est de créer des environnements à haute valeur architecturale en fonction des souhaits du client, des conditions du site et du budget du projet. L'ambition est de suivre toutes les étapes du projet, de l'esquisse au suivi de la construction, afin de mettre en oeuvre les idées architecturales dans les moindres détails.

Margen Wigow Arkitektkontor AB se inició en 2000 y está dirigido por Cecilia Margen Wigow arquitecto SAR / MSA. La oficina se especializa en villas nuevas y renovadas y casas de vacaciones. Nos impulsa la satisfacción del trabajo y un interés genuino en la arquitectura. El objetivo es crear ambientes de alto valor arquitectónico basado en los deseos del cliente, las condiciones del lugar y el presupuesto del proyecto. La ambición es seguir todas las etapas del proyecto desde el boceto hasta el seguimiento de la construcción para llevar a cabo las ideas arquitectónicas hasta el nivel de detalle.

P. 214

PAVE ARCHITECTS

www.pavearkkitehdit.fi

PAVE Architects, led by Pave Mikkonen, is a high-profile design office from Finland specialized in creating innovative and comprehensive architecture and interior design, all with their very own twist and without compromises on aesthetics.
PAVE Architects aspires to create unique buildings and sustainable environments, high in terms of quality, atmosphere and architecture, carried out with a cost-conscious and responsible service of the client. The open-minded, unprejudiced attitude, as well as the bold questioning of well-established ideas and solutions, is the core for creating and reaching new, better designs. The relationship between buildings in their broader context, such as the local conditions and environment, gives each project an individual starting point. Therefore, with PAVE Architects, each project becomes unique as the designs stem from a clean slate.

PAVE Architects, unter der Leitung von Pave Mikkonen, ist ein hochkarätiges Designbüro aus Finnland, das sich auf die Schaffung innovativer und umfassender Architektur und Innenarchitektur spezialisiert hat, die alle ihren ganz eigenen Stil hat und keine Kompromisse bei der Ästhetik eingeht.
PAVE Architects strebt danach, einzigartige Gebäude und nachhaltige Umgebungen zu schaffen, die sich durch hohe Qualität, Atmosphäre und Architektur auszeichnen und mit einem kosten- und verantwortungsbewussten Service für den Kunden ausgeführt werden. Die aufgeschlossene, unvoreingenommene Haltung sowie das mutige Infragestellen etablierter Ideen und Lösungen ist der Kern für das Schaffen und Erreichen neuer, besserer Entwürfe. Die Beziehung zwischen Gebäuden in ihrem breiteren Kontext, wie etwa den örtlichen Gegebenheiten und der Umgebung, gibt jedem Projekt einen individuellen Ausgangspunkt. Daher wird bei PAVE Architects jedes Projekt einzigartig, da die Entwürfe aus einer reinen Schiefertafel stammen.

PAVE Architects, dirigé par Pave Mikkonen, est un bureau d'études finlandais très en vue, spécialisé dans la création d'une architecture et d'un design intérieur novateurs et complets, avec leur propre touche et sans compromis sur l'esthétique.
PAVE Architects aspire à créer des bâtiments uniques et des environnements durables, de grande qualité, en termes d'atmosphère et d'architecture, réalisés avec un service au client conscient des coûts et responsable. L'ouverture d'esprit et l'absence de préjugés, ainsi que la remise en question audacieuse d'idées et de solutions bien établies, sont au coeur de la création et de la réalisation de nouveaux designs de meilleure qualité. La relation entre les bâtiments dans leur contexte plus large, comme les conditions et l'environnement locaux, donne à chaque projet un point de départ individuel. Ainsi, avec PAVE Architects, chaque projet devient unique car les conceptions sont issues d'une ardoise vierge.

PAVE Architects, dirigido por Pave Mikkonen, es una oficina de diseño de alto perfil de Finlandia especializada en la arquitectura y el diseño de interiores innovadores y completos, todos con su propio giro y sin compromisos en la estética.
PAVE Arquitectos aspira a crear edificios únicos y entornos sostenibles, de alta calidad, proyectos llevados a cabo con un servicio responsable y consciente del presupuesto del cliente. La actitud abierta y sin prejuicios, así como el cuestionamiento audaz de ideas y soluciones bien establecidas, son la base para crear y alcanzar nuevos y mejores diseños. La relación entre los edificios en su contexto más amplio, como las condiciones y el entorno local, otorga a cada proyecto un punto de partida individual. En PAVE Arquitectos, cada proyecto se convierte en único ya que los diseños surgen sin requisitos predeterminados.

P. 222

RESELL+NICCA

www.resellnicca.no

Resell+Nicca is a Norwegian architecture firm based in Oslo. The office is working towards an inclusive and locally adapted architecture that respects and at the same time challenge its surroundings. A key element behind their work is a belief that first hand knowledge about historical, geographical, cultural and environmental conditions is essential in order to create meaningful architecture that relates to its surroundings. This often results in a modern twist on traditional Scandinavian building practice. Sustainable and environmentally friendly solutions that take nature into account is a fundamental part of the work, and an important premise for all concepts.

Resell+Nicca ist ein norwegisches Architekturbüro mit Sitz in Oslo. Das Büro arbeitet an einer integrativen und lokal angepassten Architektur, die ihre Umgebung respektiert und gleichzeitig herausfordert. Ein Schlüsselelement hinter ihrer Arbeit ist die Überzeugung, dass Wissen aus erster Hand über historische, geographische, kulturelle und Umweltbedingungen unerlässlich ist, um sinnvolle Architektur zu schaffen, die sich auf ihre Umgebung bezieht. Dies führt oft zu einer modernen Wendung in der traditionellen skandinavischen Baupraxis. Nachhaltige und umweltfreundliche Lösungen, die die Natur berücksichtigen, sind ein grundlegender Bestandteil der Arbeit und eine wichtige Voraussetzung für alle Konzepte.

Resell+Nicca est un cabinet d'architecture norvégien basé à Oslo. Le travail du bureau s'articule autour d'une architecture inclusive et adaptée localement qui respecte et en même temps remet en question son environnement. Un élément clé de leur travail est la conviction qu'une connaissance de première main des conditions historiques, géographiques, culturelles et environnementales est essentielle pour créer une architecture significative en relation avec son environnement. Cela se traduit souvent par un changement de la pratique traditionnelle scandinave en matière de construction. Des solutions durables et écologiques qui tiennent compte de la nature constituent une partie fondamentale du travail et une prémisse importante pour tous les concepts.

Resell+Nicca es un estudio de arquitectura noruego con sede en Oslo. La oficina está trabajando en una arquitectura inclusiva y adaptada localmente que respete y al mismo tiempo desafíe su entorno. Un elemento clave detrás de su trabajo es la creencia de que el conocimiento de primera mano sobre las condiciones históricas, geográficas, culturales y ambientales es esencial para crear una arquitectura significativa que se relacione con su entorno. Esto a menudo da lugar a un giro moderno en la práctica tradicional de la construcción escandinava. Las soluciones sostenibles y respetuosas con el medio ambiente que tienen en cuenta la naturaleza son una parte fundamental del trabajo y una premisa importante para abordar todos los proyectos.

P. 236

STINESSEN ARKITEKTUR

www.snorrestinessen.com

Stinessen is committed to developing projects that are conscious of our surroundings and the people inhabiting the spaces we create. Interest, respect and curiosity are keywords to our processes. The studio provides a full range of services from architecture to interior and furniture design. We deliver tailor-made projects and products through a close interaction and dedicated service to our clients.

Stinessen setzt sich dafür ein, Projekte zu entwickeln, die sich unserer Umgebung und der Menschen, die die von uns geschaffenen Räume bewohnen, bewusst sind. Interesse, Respekt und Neugier sind Schlüsselbegriffe für unsere Prozesse. Das Atelier bietet eine umfassende Palette von Dienstleistungen von der Architektur bis zum Innen- und Möbeldesign. Wir liefern maßgeschneiderte Projekte und Produkte durch eine enge Interaktion und engagierten Service für unsere Kunden.

Stinessen s'engage à développer des projets qui sont conscients de notre environnement et des personnes qui habitent les espaces que nous créons. L'intérêt, le respect et la curiosité sont les mots clés de nos processus. Le studio offre une gamme complète de services allant de l'architecture au design d'intérieur et de mobilier. Nous livrons des projets et des produits sur mesure grâce à une interaction étroite et un service dédié à nos clients.

Stinessen se compromete a desarrollar proyectos que sean conscientes con el entorno y de las personas que habitan los espacios que creamos. El interés, el respeto y la curiosidad son palabras clave en nuestros procesos. El estudio ofrece una gama completa de servicios desde la arquitectura hasta el diseño de interiores y mobiliario. Entregamos proyectos y productos a medida a través de una estrecha interacción y un servicio dedicado a nuestros clientes.

P. 258

TRIGUEIROS ARCHITECTURE

www.trigueiros.net

Trigueiros Architecture is an architectural design studio based in Stockholm since 2003. We develop extraordinary and highly innovative architecture, combining contemporary flavors, international ambitions, and a true Scandinavian heritage. We always strive for results and simplicity, using Sensibility, Playfulness and Honesty as value creation basics. We design in high international standard adding values and durability. Each project being completed from sketch to ensuring craftsmanship on site. Assignments include private villas, furniture design, residential areas, commercial space etc. Architect Vasco Trigueiros originates from Brazil & Sweden runs the company with Maria Sigeman Trigueiros. Together with their team of highly dedicated colleges, the experience of projects runs scales from interior design to property development.

Trigueiros Architecture ist ein Architekturbüro mit Sitz in Stockholm seit 2003. Wir entwickeln außergewöhnliche und innovative Architektur, die zeitgenössische Einflüsse, internationale Ambitionen und ein echtes skandinavisches Erbe vereint. Unser Fokus liegt auf konkreten Ergebnissen und Einfachheit. Sensibilität, Spiel und Ehrlichkeit sind für uns grundlegende Prinzipien zur Schaffung von Mehrwert. Mit einem systematischen und präzisen Ansatz arbeiten wir eng mit unseren Kunden und ihren Visionen zusammen und begleiten jedes Projekt von der ersten Skizze bis zur handwerklichen Umsetzung vor Ort. Unsere Projekte umfassen private Villen, Möbeldesign, Wohngebiete, Geschäftsräume und mehr. Der Architekt Vasco Trigueiros, mit brasilianischen und schwedischen Wurzeln, leitet das Unternehmen gemeinsam mit Maria Sigeman Trigueiros. Zusammen mit dem Team reicht ihre Erfahrung von Innenarchitektur bis zur Immobilienentwicklung.

Trigueiros Architecture est un cabinet d'architecture basé à Stockholm depuis 2003. Nous développons une architecture exceptionnelle et innovante, combinant influences contemporaines, ambitions internationales et véritable héritage scandinave. Nous recherchons toujours simplicité et efficacité, en utilisant la sensibilité, le jeu et l'authenticité comme principes fondamentaux pour créer de la valeur. Nous travaillons de manière méthodique et minutieuse avec nos clients et leurs visions, en menant chaque projet depuis l'esquisse jusqu'au suivi artisanal sur le terrain. Nos missions comprennent des villas privées, du design de mobilier, des projets résidentiels et commerciaux, entre autres. L'architecte Vasco Trigueiros, d'origine brésilienne et suédoise, dirige l'entreprise aux côtés de Maria Sigeman Trigueiros. Avec leur équipe, leur expertise s'étend de l'architecture d'intérieur au développement immobilier.

Trigueiros Architecture es un estudio de diseño arquitectónico con sede en Estocolmo desde 2003. Desarrollamos una arquitectura extraordinaria e innovadora, combinando influencias contemporáneas, ambiciones internacionales y un verdadero legado escandinavo. Siempre buscamos resultados y simplicidad, utilizando la sensibilidad, el juego y la honestidad como principios fundamentales en la creación de valor. Trabajamos de manera sistemática y meticulosa con nuestros clientes y sus visiones, completando cada proyecto desde el boceto hasta la supervisión del trabajo artesanal en el terreno. Nuestras asignaciones incluyen villas privadas, diseño de mobiliario, áreas residenciales, espacios comerciales, entre otros. El arquitecto Vasco Trigueiros, de origen brasileño y sueco, dirige la empresa junto con Maria Sigeman Trigueiros. Junto con el equipo, su experiencia abarca desde el diseño de interiores hasta el desarrollo inmobiliario.